Siegfried Bucher

DANGEROUS
ENCOUNTERS

Printed in Victoria, Canada

Cover photograph by Siegfried Bucher

Canadian Cataloguing in Publication Data

Bucher, Siegfried, 1925-
  Dangerous encounters

  ISBN 1-55212-408-8

  1. Seismology--Research--Nunavut--Sverdrup Channel. 2.
Geology--Nunavut--Sverdrup Channel. I. Title.
QE196.N8B82 2000   557.19'5   C00-910673-1

TRAFFORD

This book was published *on-demand* in cooperation with Trafford Publishing.
On-demand publishing is a unique process and service of making a book available for retail sale to the public taking advantage of on-demand manufacturing and Internet marketing.
On-demand publishing includes promotions, retail sales, manufacturing, order fulfilment, accounting and collecting royalties on behalf of the author.

Suite 6E, 2333 Government St., Victoria, B.C. V8T 4P4, CANADA

Phone	250-383-6864	Toll-free	1-888-232-4444 (Canada & US)
Fax	250-383-6804	E-mail	sales@trafford.com
Web site	www.trafford.com	TRAFFORD PUBLISHING IS A DIVISION OF TRAFFORD HOLDINGS LTD.	
Trafford Catalogue #00-0072		www.trafford.com/robots/00-0072.html	

10   9   8   7   6   5   4   3   2

This book is dedicated
to all those who were members
of this scientific exploration
and made it a success.

FOREWORD

After several years of working as engineer I quit
that field of activity and decided to become explorer,
my true calling. But it proved to be difficult to
find work as explorer and for three years I held down
different jobs, anything but engineering. Then my
persistence was rewarded: I could join a scientific
exploration in Baffin Island. This was the beginning
of my enduring fascination with the Northland, primar-
ily the high-Arctic — its inexplicable lure entrapped
me.

And so, in 1963, I joined another scientific exploration, but this time on the ice-covered offshores in
the Queen Elizabeth Islands of the arctic archipelago.

The following story is about that exploration. It
is not a scientific essay or just another adventure
book. It is a reconstruction of an arctic exploration
that can never be restored or repeated in the way it
was conducted, nor in its significance as a scientific
endeavor — it was a first and only.

The main theme of the story revolves around the
ways this remote and, at that time, mostly unexplored
part of the Arctic affected me: the loneliness, the
cold, the harsh beauty, the physical and mental stress
I endured, and the addictive effect the Arctic had on
me. I had intended to live and to work there for a

time only, but found myself drawn back year after year.

I had wanted a chance to explore, not to live adventurously, but things happened to me that were stranger and often more exciting and frightening than anything I could have imagined. There were moments when I hated to be out there alone, endangered by all kinds of perils, and wished to see another human's face. Yet there were times when I was truly happy treading new ground and struggling against all odds nature has in store for the person exposing himself to her relentless moods. At such times I felt that nothing else can match exploration, especially exploration of the Arctic.

In the following story I describe the different arctic offshore condition I saw with complete honesty and variety within, of course, the limits of my observations, and what effect they had on my senses. I write about encounters with animals, some harmless, others extremely dangerous. And I write about the interaction of myself with my colleagues and my crew, to all of whom I had to prove myself.

To refresh my memory I have used the diary I kept during that time. And I have used dialogue to liven up the narrative and to add to character development. The dialogue is not an exact quotation, but is remarks and discussions, outbursts of anger, delight or sur-

prise that retain some of the state of mind or mood
the particular individual was in at the time.

The radio was the only means we had for long distance and air-to-ground communication. I have writ-
ten these communications in the mode we transmitted
them. (This mode has changed little, if at all, in
the meantime).

To write about how and what my companions felt
would be presumptuous of me. Only at rare occasions
did the one or the other reveal his innermost feelings. We were not psychiatrists trying to analyze
each other — we took each other the way we were and
tried to live and to work together as best we could.
Frictions, but also harmony among us were facts.

I have not used the name INUIT, today considered
politically correct in Canada, but was ESKIMO in 1963
when the exploration I write about took place. INUIT
is the plural of INUK (man), the Eskimo calls himself
in comparison with other races. The name ESKIMO is
of Algonquian origin, akin to Cree ASKIMOWEW, and
means: he eats it raw.

The places and actions I have described in these
pages are based on facts.

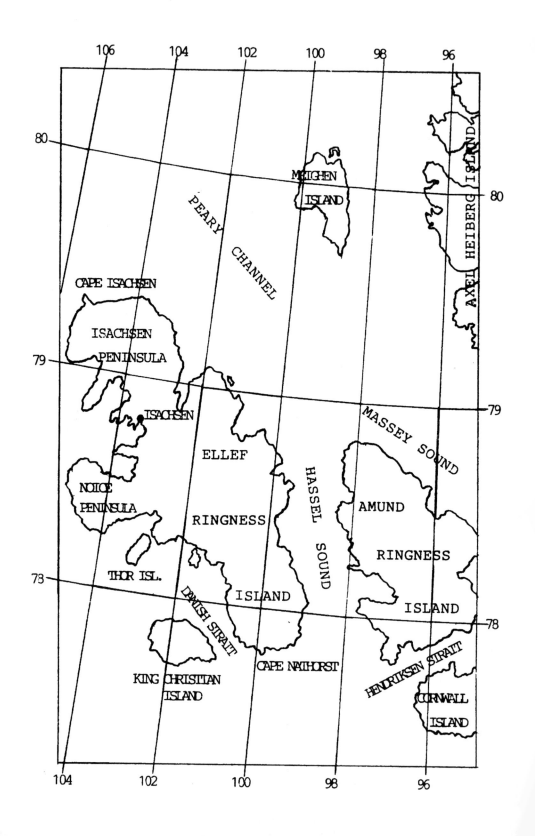

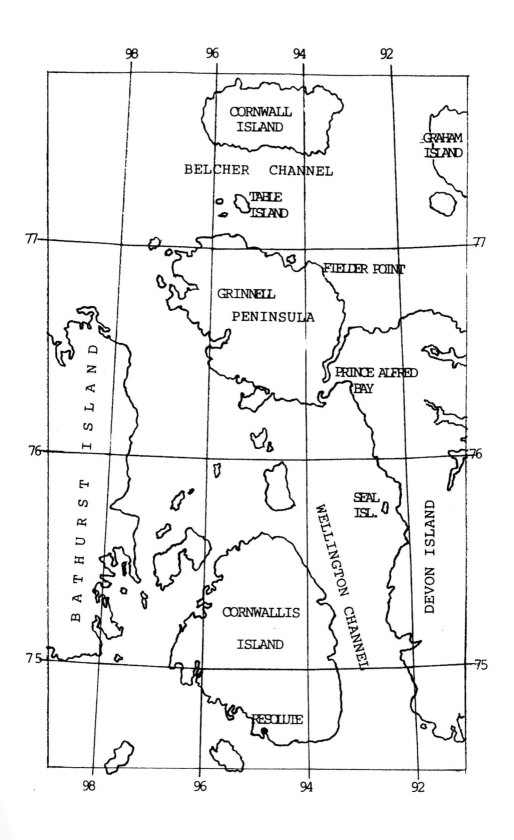

Have you strung your soul to silence? Then
    for God's sake go and do it;
Hear the challenge, learn the lesson,
    pay the cost.

                                Robert Service

CHAPTER 1

The wintry countryside was moonlit and it was close
to midnight when our car got stuck in a deep snowdrift
about fifty yards from the parking lot at the edge of
the wood through which a short trail led to our cabin
— nine miles east of Edmonton.

"Let's walk to it. I'm too tired to shovel now," I
said to Nelly, my wife.

We changed our shoes to snow-boots, zipped up the
parkas and, each shouldering a sleeping bag, floundered
through knee-high snow to the cabin.

"The bulb's burned out. I'll light a candle," I
said after I had turned on and off the light switch
several times.

Nelly sniffed the air. "Smells musty," she said,
and looking at the floor, added: "And there's mice
around."

I saw a few droppings. "Nothing to worry about.
I'll take care of 'em tomorrow," I returned, pulled
the wall-bed down and spread out the sleeping bags.

She murmured something about me having been too
long in the Arctic.

Yes ... I had been in the Arctic. Too long? I
knew she did not mean it, and I would not have agreed,
anyway.

Two weeks earlier we had left Ottawa where we had
stayed with friends after my return from Baffin Island
in September.

Daylight had not broken yet when I began to dig out
the car. The snow was powdery making the digging easy.
I was just beginning to clear away a second drift when
the snowplow came down the road. "Good to see you're
back! Was here two days ago!" the operator shouted,
leaning out of the cab.

I did not have to shovel any longer.

Next day was Christmas. A blizzard blew across the
stubble fields and howled through the woods. A fire
crackled in the fireplace and wax candles burnt brightly
on the small, decorated spruce tree. It was peaceful
and cozy in our cabin. "It's good to be home," Nelly
said, and I agreed.

After New Year we visited our neighbor, an old pro-
spector who lived by himself in a cabin, one and a half
mile from ours. He appeared to be pleased that we
looked in on him and asked us to stay for coffee.
After some remarks about the prevailing weather and
that all signs pointed at a severe and long winter, he
asked Nelly to tell him how she had fared during my
absence.

"You see, I told you she would do all right," he
said to me after he had listened attentively to her
story.

"I never said a word to the contrary," I declared.

"I know. But you worried that she cain't cope with
every kind of problems."

"No such thing!" I protested.

"Now don't get riled. Ain't no harm in worryin'. Shows that you care."

"And that he does," Nelly threw in and smiled, happily.

"Yeah, I know. I'm just teasin' him," he returned and chuckled. Then he asked me to tell about my time in the Arctic.

Silence fell after my rather enthusiastic description of my experiences. He stared at me thoughtfully, slightly troubled it seemed. "It got you ... you're charmed, my boy ... and you cain't never shake it no more," he said at length, then turned to Nelly and asked: "When's he goin' again?"

"We haven't planned anything. I might not go at all," I said before she could reply.

"Well, well. We'll see, ain't we?" he drawled.

We left him with the promise to visit again.

"As you said: we haven't planned anything," Nelly remarked while she fastened the harness of her snowshoes to her moccasins. Then, straightening up, she added, softly: "But you're thinking about it."

"How d'you know?"

She smiled. "It's easy to see. You're preoccupied and restless."

"You're right. I don't know what to do. It's a curse," I said.

"No! It isn't!" she objected. "You just have to make up your mind, that's all!"

I had received an offer to join a deep-refraction seismic survey on the ice-covered offshores of the Sverdrup Basin in the Queen Elizabeth Islands of the arctic archipelago. The aim was to determine the shape of the earth crust and the thickness of sedimentation underlying this basin. It was a scientific project planned by the Seismology Branch of the Department of Mines and Technical Surveys. 'Your task would be to operate a mobile recording station on the ice, something to be tried out for the first time', the offer stated.

Back at our cabin, Nelly and I discussed the offer.

"I think this expedition could be a great challenge, but not without dangers," I remarked.

"I know," she said with a concerned expression in her eyes. "You will be careful, won't you?"

And that settled it — I decided to join the survey. It meant a long, painful separation for both of us.

"I'll dig a garden and plant all kinds of vegetables. It will keep me busy and you'll have much greens to eat after your return," she said in answer to my question what she had in mind to do during my absence.

"Are you worried that I might get scurvy?"

"With no fresh vegetables to eat for months on end? Yes ... a bit."

Not making light of it, I assured her that getting scurvy was only a slight possibility. We also promised each other to write often.

Since the survey was not to begin before March, and our savings were almost gone, I went to work for a friend of mine who was an engineering consultant in Edmonton and had much design work he gladly left for me to do. I worked throughout the week and on weekends Nelly and I skied or snowshoed or socialized with our friends and acquaintances.

Then, around mid-March, she drove me to the airport — I was leaving for Ottawa. During thirteen hours I sat in the aircraft, listened to its droning engines, ate food I did not like and gazed down at the still wintry looking parkland of Alberta, the prairies of Saskatchewan and Manitoba, and the seemingly endless forests of Ontario.

It was close to midnight when I arrived at the airport outside Montreal and was met by George, the leader of the team of which I was a member now. It was the first time we met.

"The flight to Resolute is delayed," he said after the customary handshake.

"We're not going to Ottawa first?"

He looked at me with a tired expression in his light-blue eyes. "No. I made reservations at a hotel," he said and, smiling weakly, added: "I'm just recovering from the flu."

I did not asked why the change of plans, was, however, glad not having to board another aircraft right away.

He was an inch or two short of my five foot eleven, but heavier set. I reckoned him to be in his mid-thirties. Somehow I felt that he was a man inclined to be unyielding in his views, possibly dogmatic. He spoke with a slight German accent.

Shortly before noon we left the hotel by taxi. The weather in the north had improved; a blizzard had been the reason for the delay, I had found out.

"Give it your best," George said to the cabby.

The traffic was heavy, the roads were icy. And everybody is driving like they were maniacs, I thought and tried not to watch. At the airport the cabby grinned as he handed me my bags. "You looked scared. I bet you're not from around here," he said.

"That's for sure," I replied, then followed George through the automatic door.

"Good afternoon, Doctors," the clerk at the ticket counter greeted.

I was delighted being called Doctor and at once surprised, for George instantly corrected: "He's not Doctor, but I am."

The clerk's eyes widened. "I'm sorry, Doctor," he said and, seemingly embarrassed, glanced at me.

"He's absolutely right," I said and smiled.

10

George turned to me. "It's just for the record,
you know."

"Of course," I replied with a grin.

He blushed slightly and turned away.

The takeoff was postponed — for mechanical problems with an engine, we were told. When the cowlings
were back in place daylight had faded and we were
asked to return early next morning.

We returned before sunrise, but the flight was
again delayed by several hours.

"Ladies and gentlemen, be patient," the announcer
informed, using the habitual phrase.

There were no ladies present, only about a dozen
men of whom some smoked, some chewed gum or tobacco.
They were a taciturn group and had one thing in common: their eyes held bored expressions.

Once en route, the pilot was forced to land the
DC-6 at the airstrip near Fort Chimo. "We're holding
for the weather to improve farther north," he announced over the intercom.

I followed a few passengers to a small one-room,
wooden building that served as the heated waiting
room. A large crowd of Eskimos had gathered in it
because the arrival of a large aircraft was apparently an exciting event for young and old who had come
from their nearby settlement.

"Why so pale?" George asked when I returned to my

seat beside him. He had stayed in the aircraft during the almost two hours wait.

"Stunk like hell in that building," I replied.

He grinned mischievously. "I know. Went there once and promised myself never to do it again. Experience, eh?"

It was a bumpy flight to Frobisher Bay (today called: Irkaluit) and many a guy's face changed from bored expression to sickly looking, and each, so affected, reached for the small paper bag in the pocket of the seat in front, sooner or later.

"You smell like a dandy," George remarked, handing his bag to the purser.

"Experience, eh?" I mocked, holding my handkerchief, sprinkled with 'Eau de Cologne', to my nose a few moments longer.

"A smart thing to do," the purser said, bending his head in my direction. "There will be a refueling stop," he added.

The last leg of the flight was smooth and we arrived at Resolute after dark. Once a weather station only, Resolute was now a settlement with government agencies, a R.C.M.P. detachment, a post office and a school, and relocated Eskimos from a more southerly part of the country. The population in 1963 was 86 Eskimos and 165 Whites.

Thirty-six below zero and a strong breeze made it

very cold. Toting my two duffle bags, I made it to the entrance of the building through which I had seen most passengers disappear just in time to escape frostbite to my face.

"Can't you be more careful?" a gruff voice exclaimed. I had slammed the door shut without checking whether somebody was following me.

"I'm sorry. I didn't mean to ...," I started to apologize, but was stopped by: "Doggone, it's you!"

"Arne?" I probed, peering at a husky fellow through the dim light. (Arne and I had been members of an expedition to Baffin Island the previous year).

"Yeah, old buddy. What in heaven's name are you doing here?"

Gladness flooded me. "Could ask the same about you," I said and shook his hand. "Thought you were back in Norway."

"Was for the winter," he returned, then told me that he was working for the Polar Continental Shelf Project doing research farther north; that he was already a month stationed at Isachsen and had come to Resolute to pick up additional gear and supplies.

"But tell me: what does your wife say about you leaving her alone again?" he asked then.

"She understands," I said.

He smiled, wistfully, it seemed. "I wish I could say the same," he returned.

We walked down the hallway to the lobby of the station's building complex. "That's where you check in," Arne said, putting my bags in front of the reception desk. "Ring the bell. Someone will come."

"Thank you, Arne."

"That's all right. See you tomorrow," he replied and left.

Whether there were no bunks vacant within the building or George's budget, government funds, did not allow to rent one for me, I did not know, for no sooner had I mentioned my name and affiliation to the clerk who had appeared with a sullen look on his pudgy face after my insistent ringing of the bell, was I met by a stocky fellow clad in polar wear and whose face was hidden under a frosted balaclava. He grabbed my bags, said: "Come," and walked away. The clerk answered my questioning look at him with a nod and a slighting grin.

I followed the fellow down the same hallway whence I had come with Arne, and through the door into the open. I was stung by the cold again as we walked behind each other along an uneven path in the snow to a small prefab building some distance from the station.

"You here," the fellow said, dropped the bags onto the lower sleeping platform of a bunk, turned around and left, slamming the metal door shut. His squeaking footsteps faded — I was alone.

An electric bulb hung from the ceiling. It dimly

lit two rooms: a large one, apparently used as kitchen
and office, and a small one containing two double
bunks. An oil-fired space heater hummed at full blast.
Its heat had melted the thick hoarfrost that covered
the walls halfway down their sides. It felt as if I
had stuck my head into the Desert while standing in
the Arctic.

"It's good my bunk's in the cold region," I muttered, rolled out the sleeping bag, undressed, shivered
as my naked body made contact with the cold liner of
the bag, then fell asleep.

"Nice to have an easy job," Arne remarked as we met
in the morning for a late breakfast in the dining room.
He had been up before daybreak and had already loaded
the aircraft which would take him back to Isachsen.

"It won't be so easy once I'm on the ice," I said.

He nodded. "I heard you'll be sledging with an
Eskimo."

"Yes. And an Indian will be my helper. But where
did you hear that?"

"At the bar when I had a beer . Some guys were
talking about you. They sounded like they know you."

"Did you ask 'em who they are and who told 'em?"

"No, I didn't. But tell me: do the two guys speak
English or French? Something you understand."

"Really I don't know. I've never even thought
about that," I admitted.

He grinned. "It might be fun ... three guys, each speaking a language the others don't understand."

"If this is the case, we'll work it out," I made light of it, but was not so sure it would be an easy thing to do.

He looked at the clock on the wall. "It's getting late. I must leave. Have to pack my bags," he said, got up and, his eyes sparkling prankishly, went on: "Watch yourself. Where you're heading for there's bears around. They might not like you."

"Thanks for telling me. You're a real pal," I kidded, but did not feel at ease, somehow.

After he had left I went looking for George. I found him in his room; the number I got from the clerk.

"Where the heck were you?" he snapped and, without waiting for me to reply, thrust some papers at me. "Read them. They'll give you an idea what we'll be doing and how."

I made for a chair to sit down and to read them.

"Not now! You can do that later!" he barked while he put on his parka. "Follow me!" he ordered.

We left the station via its main entrance and walked to the prefab building I had spent the night in. Two Indians, busy with putting on their footwear, sat on the floor in the large room. In the night they had awakened me with their clamor. They had smelled of booze, and I had pretended to be asleep. Their

utterances I had recognized as Cree. In the morning,
when I had risen, both had been fast asleep.

"You've met them, haven't you?" George asked in an
undertone.

"No, I haven't," I returned.

"This is Teddy," he said aloud with a nod at the
younger of the two. "He'll be your helper."

"Hi, Teddy," I greeted. "You're the fellow who
brought me here, right?"

"Yes," he replied in a level voice. I saw no emotion in his dark eyes nor on his face, its striking
features a short, broad nose and wide cheekbones.

"And this is Guss," George said.

I greeted Guss.

"I'm Tony's helper," he said, also in a level voice.
"I'm Teddy's uncle and ...." He stopped speaking be-
cause interrupting him, George said to me: "You and
Teddy may as well start digging out your equipment."

He opened the door and pointed at a large snowdrift
to one side of the path. "It's all there," he said
with a grin, obviously enjoying my consternation.

"What? There? I can't believe ...," I started,
changed my mind, and asked: "Where do I move it to?"

"Just dig it out and leave it where it is," he replied, turned to Teddy and told him to help me. "You
come along with me," he said to Guss, then left. "You
know where to get your meals!" he called from a distance.

The snowdrift was hard-packed and deep. It took us almost two days to dig out the equipment. Late afternoon of the second day a strong wind began to blow, and the following morning the equipment was buried again under several feet of snow.

I cursed. Teddy did not utter a word — his facial expression remained stoical. We dug again, but this time moved the equipment into the lee of the building.

"Why not do before?" Teddy said. It was the first complete sentence he spoke since we had begun to work. Initially, I had wanted to strike up conversations, but his short 'nos' and 'yeses' had let me to believe that he could neither understand nor speak English well, and so I had stopped trying. Now, I was surprised and at once relieved. "Ah, you speak English," I said.

"Went to mission. Learn there," he returned.

I wanted to know more, but curbed my curiosity. There will be plenty of time for that, I decided.

We had almost finished digging out when George appeared. He did not greet, but stood still and with his eyes searched the piled up equipment. I'm sure he's looking for the instruments, I thought and out loud I said: "They're inside ... thawing out."

He gaped. "How did you ... that is ... are they damaged?" he stammered.

"I don't know yet. They should never have been

left in the open," I replied.

We both wore tuques. He had his pulled down to his brows, yet I saw him redden. I got a hunch. "It was you, wasn't it?" I queried.

"I can't remember," he said, turned around and left.

"Him not say," Teddy remarked.

Four days later all equipment, food and fuel we were to need during the first few weeks on the ice were assembled. I had serviced, repaired and tested the instruments of which all plugs and most contacts had been badly corroded. They functioned properly again.

All fired up by the prospect of sledging across the frozen sea, something I had dreamed about since boyhood, I told George that I was ready to load up and leave.

"There's no need for that now. You and Teddy must go with Bill to set up Tony's camp and recording station," he said.

He had mentioned Tony and Bill before, and Guss had said that he was Tony's helper. They were the two scientists who were to operate semi-permanent recording stations each. I had not met them yet, but knew that Tony had just recovered from a bout of pneumonia and was still weak. Though I recognized the need for the change of plans, I was still disgruntled. "What about my schedule?" I demanded.

19

"That won't change," he said. My stuff would be
flown to a small island off the coast of Devon Island
and halfway up Wellington Channel. Teddy and I were
to fly there and commence our task after we had set
up Tony's camp.

"Andrew will join you there. I told him to come
and see you today," he added, turned away, yet after
a few steps came back and said with a grin: "I'm sure
you'll be thanking me for shortening your trip by dogsled."

"Why should I?"

"Because you'll be sick of it at the end of the
season."

I did not reply to that, but thought with conviction: that won't happen.

Teddy and I were leveling the piles of snow we had
thrown up when digging out our equipment and supplies,
when an Eskimo came from the station. He was short —
five foot one or two, I reckoned. He wore sealskin
kamiks and over a creamy duffle shirt a dark-green
anorak with pointed hood and adorned with colored ribbons. The hood was trimmed with white fur that partly
hid his face. His hands stuck in mittens of native
tailoring.

He approached to within a few paces, stood still
and silently watched us. His eyes were dark. I'm
sure it's Andrew, I thought, but having lost the habit

of white man to greet and introduce oneself at the
instant of meeting, I was at ease and waited for him
to make verbal contact.

"Me ... Andrew," he said at length.

Good, he speaks English, I thought, greatly relieved, and said my name. Teddy said his. We shook
hands then. Apparently satisfied with that, Andrew
said: "Nâmaktok," turned on his heels and strode back
whence he had come.

"Wait! I want to talk with you!" I called.

It seemed that he did not hear me, so I shouted:
"Come back! And let's talk!"

He turned his head and nodded with a broad smile,
but kept walking away from us. I did not know what
to make of it.

"Mebee, him not talk English," Teddy remarked, instantly reminding me of Arne's remark about three guys
not understanding each other's language. "It might
be fun," I muttered, repeating what Arne had said.

Teddy looked at me, but his face did not betray
what he was thinking.

I laughed. "Never you mind what I said," I declared.

George advised me to visit Tony in his room. "Do
it after supper and you'll find Bill with him, he said.

He was right — Bill was there. Both seemed to know
who I was, for Tony, his face still showing traces of

his recent illness, looked me over with tired eyes, whereas Bill, his eyes squeezed to mere slits, scrutinized me for long moments before he seemed to approve of me. "Sit down," he said at length and pointed at an empty chair. "So you're the one who'll run the small recorder on the ice," he went on and grinned. He looked at Tony. "Can you imagine doing that?"

"Not really," Tony replied with a weak smile.

Apprehension gripped me. "What do you two mean by that?" I queried.

"That it might be tough going for you ... right, Tony?" Bill responded.

"Yes," Tony said, and after a moment, "has George told you what you'll be up against out there?"

"Are you two trying to scare me?"

"Not at all. We just want you to know that your job won't be easy, but very important for us," Bill returned.

"You won't be sorry to have me on your team ... I promise you that," I said with conviction.

"I rather like that," Bill said and got up. And now I saw that he topped me at least by two inches and was of powerful built. "See you tomorrow," he said to Tony, then turned to me. "Are you coming?"

"Come again. We'll talk some more," Tony said. He sounded tired.

I visited him a few more times, alone and in company of Bill. We talked about the pending work, the possible problems we might encounter, and how to combat or alleviate them. We got to know each other, and since both had worked seismic in the Arctic and in other parts of the country, I profited from their experience they freely related to me.

CHAPTER 2

On the last day in March, Bill, Teddy and I left
Resolute by single-engine aircraft, a de-Havilland
Otter. The sun's orbit above the southern horizon
had lengthened to almost two-thirds of his daily
journey across the northern sky. Yet this celestial
body sent no perceptible warmth — the air was a
frigid thirty-eight below zero, and a steady breeze
made it the colder. Our breath, white streaks of
vapor, settled as hoarfrost on the fur-trimmings of
our parkas and woolen face masks.

"The cabin won't be heated," Dale, the pilot,
said. "So make it out among yourselves who wants
to sit up front."

He wore sunglasses and was dressed in bulky arctic clothes, giving him the semblance of a spaceman.
That he was of my height, I could see, but whether
he was of light built or heavy set and what his age
was, I could have only guessed.

"I'll do it!" Bill declared. "You guys are
tougher than I," he added, an insolent grin in his
fleshy face.

I silently cursed him because it was to be my
first flight in a small aircraft across the high-
arctic land I yearned to see, and sitting up front,
in the co-pilot's seat, would have given me unob-

structed view. Disappointed, I climbed into the cabin. The windows were frosted. I scratched a peep-
hole on the one I sat next to and when we reached
cruising altitude I watched eagerly the features of
the benumbed land and sea which passed below.

It was a mosaic of thousand shapes and sizes, all
drawn in black and white with a bluish hue. The
scenery was sunlit. The snow sparkled and the odd
patches of open water or bare ice glared. Shadows,
narrow and long-stretched in places, broad and short
in others, revealed spires, cliffs and ridges which
otherwise would not have been distinguishable from
the air. And all shadows pointed north and, with the
sun's orbit, grew short, then long again while veer-
ing slowly eastward.

We had crossed the southern shore of the Grinnell
Peninsula when Dale suddenly banked the aircraft and
flew a tight circle.

"See the muskoxen?" he shouted above the roar of
the engine, and pointed.

With the palm of my hand I melted a clear spot on
the pane, peered, felt disappointed ... then saw the
shaggy beasts. They were a herd of eleven adults and
three young. Obviously alarmed by the aircraft's
droning they stampeded short distance, stopped and
formed a circle, their massive, horned heads low and
facing out. The young were in the center of their

defensive array. I had seen muskoxen at game farms, but never before in the wild. I was thrilled!

Dale turned his head and gave a nod which I answered with a nod. He leveled the wings and bore toward Fielder Point on the north shore of the peninsula where he made a smooth landing on a level strip of windblown snow.

The immediate surroundings were littered with boxes, crates, fuel barrels, parts of masts and tubing for tent frames. It showed that several loads had been hurriedly dumped without always taxiing the aircraft to the same spot. Some things were part of long snowdrifts, others lay in windblown moulds.

While the three of us unloaded, Dale let the engine run, for shutting it off in the prevailing cold could have rendered it difficult, if not impossible, to restart without an external heater, an item we had not on board.

A short time later we watched the aircraft climb into the pale-blue sky and slowly fade from sight.

"He'll be back tomorrow," Bill remarked, rubbing his frostbitten nose and cheeks with the furpad on the back of his gauntlets. He did not wear a balaclava like Teddy and I.

"You guys are good," he said a few hours later. He sat, hunched forward, on a cot and pensively sipped tea from a mug.

The tent was up and banked high with snowblocks

cut from hard-blown drifts. Its floor space, twelve
by sixteen feet, was covered with sheets of plywood.

"Will I have such a floor in my tent?" I asked.

His brown eyes lit up and he smiled. "You would
like that, wouldn't you?"

"Of course."

"You know George, don't you?"

"Not really ... why?"

"He's the one who says what goes and what not. And
I don't think you're on the list for such luxury."

"Are you?"

"Nope!" he said with finality in his voice, giving
me the impression that there was no love lost between
the two, so to say.

There was silence save for the murmur of the space
heater radiating pleasant warmth, and the low whine
of the breeze in the guy ropes of the tent.

The light began to wane. Teddy got up — he had
lain on his sleeping bag spread across a few boxes —
and with a flick of his right thumb lit a match which
he touched to the glow mantle of the fuel lamp hang-
ing on a piece of wire tied to the ridge pole of the
tent. With his left hand he turned the knob, a hissing sound arose, there was a flicker, a flame shot
up, the hissing became louder and the mantle began to
glow. He lowered the glass cover and turning the knob,
adjusted the brightness. The inner of the tent was

lighted. Then he rolled a cigarette. "Cook now?" he asked.

"Sure," Bill and I chorused.

In the morning a cloudless, sunlit sky greeted us. The breeze had died down and though it was forty-two below zero, the cold did not sting.

We laid out four miles of recording cable to which we connected large and heavy geophones. It was hard labor, and not before way past noon were we done with it.

At three o'clock Dale was back with a load of crates and boxes containing groceries for Tony.

After Bill had closed the cargo door he climbed into the co-pilot's seat. "See you guys!" he shouted. He was leaving for his station, the other semi-permanent recording site.

"I'll fetch you and Teddy around noon tomorrow!" Dale called from the cockpit window as I gave him the sign that all was clear.

Next morning dense fog wafted back and forth; its breath was so gentle that the windmeater did not rotate. Hoarfrost hung on guys and antenae and adorned masts, the tent and the piles of staples. It was phantasmal scenery intensified by faint, weird noises which resembled groans, rumbles and splashes. At times, these eerie sounds strengthened, the windmeter began to rotate and the ground took on shape. But

before the white veil ripped asunder and the surroundings were swept clear of fog by a breeze, the
sounds grew faint again, the meter slowed, stopped
turning, and the ground lost its features.

"I bet there's open water nearby," I said, thinking aloud as I contemplated the various sounds.

"Looks soaked in at your place. Can't pick you
up," the VHF radio emitted suddenly.

Teddy left the tent. I grabbed the microphone.
"Read you loud and clear. Is it you, Dale? — over."

"Yes. I'm returning to Resolute. See you tomorrow, — over."

"Affirmative. Fielder Point standing by," I transmitted and laid the microphone down.

"Only hear. No see him," Teddy said as he returned
from the outside.

During two more days fog lay over the land and sea.
Then the windmeter began to rotate, a breeze picked
up, the fog dissolved and overhead a few stars twin-
kled in the nightly sky. By morning the breeze was
strong and heavy ground drift slowly buried the supplies left in the open. We stayed in the tent. Teddy
had found paperbacks and magazines in a box. I read
a 'Western', he leafed through magazines.

"Aren't you interested in the stories?" I asked.

"No read English," he replied.

This surprised me, for I had seen him make the sign

of the cross, then read in a black book before turning in.

"But I saw you read yesterday evening," I said.

"It is bible," he explained.

"Then you can read?"

"Only Cree," he replied and handed me the bible.
It was printed in Syllabic.

"Didn't they teach you the English alphabet at the
mission?"

"Yes. I forgot," he said, the shade of a smile on
his lips.

Since the camp was to remain at the existing location during several weeks, we built a latrine out of
snowblocks, and equipped it with a metal bucket lined
with a plastic bag and covered with a wooden seat.
Every time I used that privy I felt that even in this
wild land I was a civilized member of the human race.

I made it a habit to check the recording line every
morning, weather permitting. There existed the possibility that arctic foxes, even polar bears, had chewed
the cable. The eight-mile hike was also a welcome
exercise. On one such occasion I encountered four
muskoxen, perhaps twenty-five or thirty yards distant.
They had come out of nowhere, or so it seemed. Though
I was uneasy, their presence thrilled me and I edged
closer until one began to rub its head against a foreleg and took a step in my direction. The beast was

almost five foot tall. A bull, I reckoned and re-
traced a few steps. Immediately the animal calmed
down; I had done the right gesture — retreated.

All had horns; massive structures that covered the
head like a shield. Broad at the forehead and aris-
ing close together, the horns curved downward along
the sides of the face behind the eyes, then upward to
a sharply tapered point. Their bodies were covered
in long, flowing, dark-brown hair that fell almost to
their fetlocks. The hoofs were broad, their humps
pronounced. They stood beside each other, their heads
lowered, their dark eyes gleaming. All appeared to be
on guard, and I did not press my luck by trying to get
closer again. I just kept watching them until the
cold crept through my wear and I began to shiver.

At nightfall the beasts still stood at the same
spot, calmly facing the wind that had sprung up, their
hair streaming back along their massive bodies. In
the morning they were gone. I had not heard a sound
of their leaving.

The wind had increased. It blew the snow in great
gusts across the land restricting visibility to a few
yards. It blew for a day and then abated. And, once
again, the monotonous landscape sparkled under a
cloudless, blue sky.

It was shortly before noon when the radio pealed:
"This is M-E-S. What's your weather? Fielder Point."

I transmitted the weather information and added:
"Watch for the recording cable. We flagged it — over."
(M-E-S were the identification letters of the aircraft
Dale was piloting).

"Will do," the radio beamed, and after a few moments:
"Coming in."

A roar passed over the tent, changed to a swish,
and shortly after we heard the rumble of the aircraft's
engine coming closer — Dale had landed and taxied to
where Teddy and I were waiting.

I climbed into the co-pilot's seat. The view was
magnificent. As I had guessed, there was open water
off the coast.

"There was more ... four days ago!" Dale shouted as
I pointed.

I knew now that the sounds I had heard had come
from the movement of the ice cover. As chance would
have it, a few days later I experienced such movement
and escaped disaster by narrow margin.

We landed at Bill's camp at the northern shore of
Prince Alfred Bay in Wellington Channel; two tents,
many barrels of fuel and a great pile of equipment.
Whether the camp was on land or on ice I could not
make out from the air, for there was no marked transition — all was smooth, level white, and only when we
had landed and I dug with my heels did I find out
that underneath was sand.

To my surprise some of the piled up equipment was mine. While we were drinking what Bill called 'Surveyor's Tea', a brew that made my heart palpitate, I asked him why my stuff was at his camp and not at the site of my first recording station.

He shrugged. "How should I know? The boss ordered it so," he said, then added with sarcasm: "It's not the first time he screwed up, so don't worry ... we'll make it right."

He told us that a bear had chewed the recording cable and made off with a part including several geophones. "We haven't found them yet," he added.

"We saw the tracks when coming in," Dale said.

"That was another bear. He came today," remarked Rick whom Bill had introduced as his helper. He sat near the space heater and when he did not cough or sip from his cup he twanged a guitar and sang with a raspy voice some verse in Gaelic.

He was a good-looking chap. His dark hair, combed straight back, fell down to the nape of his neck. His eyes were the color of coal, and a sensuous mouth softened the willfulness of his square chin.

Before I left the tent Bill asked me to lend him Teddy for a day or two.

"It will be quite a job to find that cable and repair it. And since Rick's not well I've no help," he explained.

"I understand. Teddy is yours to help," I returned.

He sighed relieved. "Thanks. I'll make it up to
you," he said, and I wondered how he would do that.

"Rick, take care. Teddy, you stay and help Bill,"
I said and left the tent.

I never saw Rick again. His cough got worse and
within a fortnight he flew south to warmer country.
But I did not know this before the end of the season
when I met Bill at Isachsen and asked him about
Rick's whereabout.

Since I was to be alone for a day or two and did
not trust the weather nor the return of the aircraft
on promised time, I made sure that all parts of my
small house tent, the cooking stove and food for
several days were loaded on board of the aircraft.
Neither Dale nor Bill showed impatience when I dug in
the pile of equipment for the box containing several
flashlights and batteries and ammunition for my rifle,
a Remington 700.

"Here, you'll need this," Bill said, hoisting up a
10-gallon barrel of Iosol. "And remember: don't kill
any bear except if you can prove self-defense. Otherwise, you might have trouble explaining it to the
authorities."

I wanted to ask why this was so, but Dale, looking
at the sun, urged: "Let's go."

It was getting late in the afternoon and, after
dropping me off at my destination, he wanted to be
back at Resolute before dark.

Some time later we landed close to the shore of
Seal Island where my first recording station was to
be. The island was so small and flat that only the
odd stretch of grounded and piled up ice and some
dark patches made it visible from the air. (Seal Island lies about two miles off the west coast of Devon
Island and some thirty odd miles south of Price
Alfred Bay).

"I'll bring you the rest of your gear early tomorrow," Dale said after we had unloaded the aircraft,
and he removed the red ribbon-flagged safety stops
that locked the elevator and rudder. He threw the
stops into the hold, locked its door, climbed into
the cockpit, started the engine, ran it up and then
took off.

The aircraft disappeared in a whirl of snow the
propeller was blowing my way. And as the snow settled I saw it climb into the sky. I stood and listened intently. The droning grew faint and then gave
way to utter silence.

I was alone! Abandoned, I thought, and a para-
lyzing feeling assailed me — I did not dare to move.

The surroundings were white and hazy-blue with a
yellow dot, the sun, near the southwesterly horizon.

The cold crept through my polar wear and bit my limbs and body. And, all of a sudden, I thought of freezing to death and of bears on the prowl. This roused me to action.

I pulled the rifle from its cover, worked its bolt a few times — I had treated it with a special lubricant for cold weather use — inserted the magazine filled with cartridges, slammed one into the chamber, set the safety and laid it onto the fuel barrel.

Then I pitched the tent and banked it high with snow. Its ten by twelve foot floor space I covered with a doubled-up tarpaulin of strong canvas. Underneath it was down-packed snow on top of ice that capped fathoms of frigid water.

It was dark when I bound the bottommost tie of the tent's entrance flap. I lit a candle, set up the cooking stove, melted snow in a pot, poured the content of a package of dehydrated chicken soup into the boiling water, added a can of corned beef and much butter. The resulting thick, greasy concoction chased the numbness from my body and the gloominess from my mind. Then I made tea sweetened with honey.

Despite the twenty below zero within the tent I relaxed, listened to the moaning wind and mused about being alone where nature is prime, implacable. In my mind I saw the land as it had appeared from the air, and conjured up a picture of its real features. I thought of dangers hidden to the inexperienced and often surprising the experienced, and of the animals I would meet, sooner or later. I thought again of bears and for a moment wished I would not be alone. Indeed, I'm a coward, I thought, half-ashamed.

After some time I rolled out the sleeping bag, disrobed, blew out the candle and snuggled down in the down-filled robe.

Hours later I awoke. My joints were aching — the cold had crept from the ice into my bedding. The remainder of the night I tossed sleeplessly, was raked with shivers, and cursed myself for having forgotten to bring a cot along.

When twilight brightened I dressed and after having been outside for a spell I cooked breakfast.

The tent was not heated — it was merely a shelter protecting me from the icy breeze. My breathing and the steam rising from the cooking pot, coated its inside with a fine layer of crystal-encrusted frost, giving it the appearance of an ice cave, an abode that did not tempt to linger.

I washed the dishes and then took a stroll across the island. The dark patches, Dale and I had seen from the air, were low, windblown ridges covered with yellow lichens and brown moss. I walked to the island's highest point, about fifty feet above the ice-covered surface of Wellington Channel. The view was

far and wide. What I saw was a cheerless white land
with shades of dark, and all together uninviting.
Yet it held a sinister lure that gripped my senses.
And I longed to travel beyond the pale-blue horizon
to find new vistas, new surprises or none of these.

It was late afternoon when I heard the steadily
increasing drone of an aircraft. I felt relieved.
For hours I had waited with increasing uneasiness for
Dale to arrive.

"I had trouble starting the engine in the morning.
That's why I'm late," he explained.

"Why's Teddy not with you?" I asked.

"They haven't found the cable yet," he replied,
then told me he would bring the rest of my stuff next
day. "And also Teddy," he added with a smile.

Again, I was alone. But I had a cot and a small
space heater now, providing the comfort I had not had
the night before. I was at ease and enjoyed the soli-
tude where only few would ever be.

It was still dark when I awoke with a start. I
felt a heave, heard groans and a heartbeat later the
sound of grinding. Alarmed, I groped for the flash-
light somewhere in my sleeping bag. In its beam I
saw no disorder in the tent; the space heater stood
on its box and hummed monotonously; every item lay
where I had put it, and yet the candle lantern hang-
ing from the ridge pole swung to and fro.

"Earthquake? Bear?" I asked, thinking aloud.
"Unlikely," I concluded.

The heaving, groaning and grinding had stopped.
What was it? I wondered, less afraid now, but curious. I dressed, untied the entrance flap and stepped into the open to gasp and stare in disbelief.
Through a layer of haze, tinted a weak red by the
glow of early morning, I saw water not more than ten
feet from the tent.

"By God! A lead!" I exclaimed, my voice hoarse,
a sickening sensation in the pit of my stomach.

I remembered having seen a crack in the ice when
I had returned from the stroll across the island.
But I had not given it a second thought. And now
the ice had parted, leaving a rent too wide for me
to jump across. It ran some distance from shore
along the island. How long it was I could not see.
Though I did not like the situation, the nameless
oppression, I dismissed rising fear and with my eyes
surveyed the immediate surroundings. The ice was
better than five feet thick — it would easily carry
the tent, my gear and myself. That was no problem.
But would it break up right under the tent? That
thought sent shivers down my spine.

The lead had cut me off from reaching land. But
I did not have to be on land.

"I must move my stuff away from it," I said to my-

self and pondered whether to do it right away or to
cook breakfast first. I decided on the latter, a decision that almost cost my life.

I was washing the dishes when, suddenly, the soapy
water spilled from the pan, the tarp-covered floor
tilted up and up and just before everything in the
tent, including myself, slid to one side I heard
cracking and the tilt reversed with a splash. Though
badly frightened, I did not panic, but acted fast and
precise. I turned off the fuel supply to the space
heater, sealed the fuel can, gathered sleeping bag
and rifle under my arm, grabbed with my right a pot
and the cooking stove and took to the open to break
my step, bewildered. The lead had closed. In its
place was a ridge of piled up ice, so high and jumbled that it defeated any attempt to traverse it.
And all of it was in motion, slow and almost sound-
less. My situation was desperate. To escape being
crushed or drowned, I had no other choice than to
flee from the ridge to where the ice was level and
appeared undisturbed.

It was no easy or safe flight, for I floundered
through deep snowdrifts, and twice my foot found no
firm surface. Both times I hurled myself forward,
fell, scrambled to my feet, gathered up the gear,
then kept hastening ahead, the first steps gingerly
probing.

I fled perhaps one hundred yards before I thought
myself safe. I deposited the load and went back to
get the tent and, if possible, the rest of the gear.
It was risky doing, but if I was to survive in case
of a weather change that would prevent Dale from flying, I had to have a shelter.

Luck was with me — I could retrieve the tent, its
frame, the space heater, and what not.

When I had set up camp again I felt the urge to
whoop. But all I did was to stare at the huge ridge
of tumbled, broken and piled up ice that could have
spelled my end, my grave.

It was shortly before noon when Dale landed with
another load of my equipment.

"When coming in I thought that something wasn't
right. But there was your tent ... and that was all
that mattered," he said.

I told him about my experience.

He shook his head. "You sure were lucky. Have
you a clue what caused that mess?"

"Not really."

"Could it be strong current or strong wind shifting the ice?"

"It's as good a guess as any other," I said and
smiled.

We left it by that.

"One more load and you'll have all your stuff," he

said, ready to climb into the cockpit.

"When will you be back?"

"Let me see ... it'll take me ... hem ...,"

"How about in two hours?" I interjected.

He gazed at me, then smiled: "All right. It's a deal. I really wanted to fly back to Res and come back tomorrow ... but I think you earned a break."

"Thanks, Dale. And tell Teddy I need him here."

"Will do," he said.

In less than two hours he returned with the rest of my equipment — and Teddy.

A few hours later I lay on my cot and watched Teddy turn the sizzling pork chops in the frying pan. We had sorted out our supplies and gear, and he was preparing our supper now.

"Dale say ... you bad time," he said, suddenly. He had not spoken a word since his arrival, and I had wondered whether something bothered him.

"It wasn't fun ... that's for sure," I said, then asked: "Does Bill know?"

His face lost the stoic expression. "Him say ... guys like you much crazy in head ... build camp much close to island ... ice move and break all time ... then him laugh ... and Rick ... and say to me good luck ... then laugh more."

I felt as if I had been ridiculed. He seemed to sense it.

42

"You no crazy," he said. "George him say you here first time ... you learn ... me learn ... me here first time."

"You're right. Experience is the best teacher," I said, then asked: "Are you afraid to stay with me?"

"No!" he declared, and I was sure that he meant it.

Two days later I was ready to record the first seismic shot of the planned traverse. The preparations had been exhausting labor. The recording cable was split into eight sections and was wound onto as many reels. Each reel thus weighted was heavy. Since the cable had to be laid out in a straight line, Teddy and I struggled through waist-high snowdrifts, slithered over patches of glare ice, broke through crusted snow, instead of zigzagging over hard-blown patches of snow that would have supported us. We fell, scrambled to gain firm footing, kneeled or sprawled spent and gasping. And the temperature was thirty-two below zero with a brisk wind blowing across a scenery that was numb, cold to the touch, downright depressing. We sweated and froze in turns, suffered the sting of frost to nose, ears and cheeks, and the fingers were stiff, unfeeling. But we did not relent until the cable, resembling a penciled black line, stretched a mile over the ice.

The next task was to plant and hook up the many geophones. Before we tackled it we took a warming-up

43

break — hot tea while standing near the space heater.

"Have you seen the toboggan?" I asked.

"Not here ... Bill him say he take."

"Dammit! Why did he have to do that?" I exploded.

"Him not say," Teddy responded promptly.

My anger gone, I laughed. "I guess not."

As we stumbled for the x-th time back to camp to fetch the last geophones to be hooked up, Teddy remarked: "Toboggan good now," and I agreed.

When I switched on the instruments, some geophones transmitted too much wind noise, others showed up dead. It took us hours to eliminate these problems. Then, and only then, did I transmit by radio: "Seismic 3 is ready and standing by to record."

A few moments passed before the loudspeaker emitted weakly: "This is Seismic 2. Good show. Congratulation."

It was Bill. Should I tell him about the toboggan? I asked myself. No! I decided.

"Seismic 1. I join that, Seismic 3. Where is the Shooting Crew? Does anyone know? — over."

That was Tony. So he's well again, I thought and was pleased.

"Thanks, guys. No, Haven't heard from them, — over," I transmitted.

"I have," Bill sent. "They'll be at your camp sometime tonight, Seismic 3. Did you get that, Seismic 1?"

"Affirmative. Seismic 1 standing by."

"Seismic 2 standing by."

"Seismic 3 standing by," I sent and put the microphone on its hook.

There was radio silence again. I was pleased that Tony and Bill had praised me for my efforts.

After eating the meal Teddy had prepared I began to read Bleak House by Charles Dickens. Although my eyes moved down the pages, I could not concentrate on the story, for the Shooting Crew was on my mind.

"Teddy, let's go and flag the line. The Shooting Crew might not see it," I said and put the book aside.

When the sun set as a red dot over the southern horizon and the bluish hue that spread over the snow began to darken, heralding a few hours of night, we had marked the line with bamboo poles from which streamed red ribbons in the breeze.

Suddenly, the low moan of the breeze was mixed with short, high-pitched yelps.

"Fox," Teddy said and pointed at fresh animal tracks. He scooped up a handful of snow. "See ... red ... blood ... mating time ... she."

"You say, you no here before," I said, falling into his jargon.

"Yes ... no here before. Me know fox ... all places same."

Having said this, he walked along the fox spoor

for a stretch, then turned toward the tent.

I hope they won't chew the cable, I thought, scanned with my eyes the dusky surroundings for a while longer, then returned to the tent, too.

The luminous arms of my watch showed half past midnight. I stood outside the tent and painted the snow with a yellow mark while watching an Aurora Borealis spread its colorful display across the nightly sky.

Suddenly, from a distance, I heard a whine that rose and fell in pitch. I cupped each ear with a hand and scanned the surroundings for the direction whence it came.

"South," I muttered. "Teddy! They're coming!" I shouted and stormed into the tent.

"Make coffee?" he asked.

"Good idea," I replied.

Minutes later the high-pitched whine of a snow-mobile drew near, became almost unbearable, then stopped abruptly. There were squeaking steps, the tent flaps parted and George, dusted with snow from head to toe, stepped in. With a quick tug he pulled off the gauntlets and mitten, threw them on the floor, flung back the hood of the parka, and yanked the frosted balaclava from his head.

"Your radio's out of tune!" he snapped, visibly annoyed.

While he rubbed his red-blotched stubbly cheeks,
his eyes roved over the contents of the tent. They
were arranged in a orderly and practical way. At the
left side and close to the entrance was my cot. On
it lay rolled up my 'Woods Five-Star' sleeping bag.
Next to the cot were stacked the instrument boxes. On
top of them sat the recording instruments and the
SSB and VHF radios. Near the rear wall stood the
space heater on a wooden pallet. Its pipe reached
straight up and vented into the open through an as-
bestos-cloth rimmed hole in the roof. In the far
right corner stood two crates with their opening facing the inner of the tent. They served as kitchen: a
two-burner camp-stove and the whole kit and caboodle
for cooking and eating. Adjoining it, was Teddy's
cot with his sleeping bag. And finally, three wooden
boxes stood in the center of the tent. They served
as table and two seats.

Having seen all, George fixed his eyes on me.

"Why didn't you answer my calls?" he rapped.

"Your calls?"

"Yes! My calls!"

"I received Tony's and Bill's, but not your's," I
asserted, then added, sharply: "Check **your** radio! It
might not work! And don't blame me!"

A dim flicker of uncertainty showed in his eyes.
He looked away and began to wipe the snow from his

clothes.

"Can't you do this outside?" I objected, hotly.

His head shot up. "You don't order ...," he started, stopped speaking, then left the tent.

I glanced at Teddy. He was settling the coffee with a piece of ice, then filled three cups to their brims. "Him ... you .. need," he remarked.

"You're right," I said and grinned.

George returned with his parka under one arm. Standing just inside the entrance flaps, he said: "They told me you're quick-tempered."

"Maybe so. But only if I'm rubbed the wrong way," I retorted.

Not wanting to quarrel because I knew that it was bad when men who depend on each other do so, I asked: "Are you hungry?"

He showed surprise. "What have you got?"

"There's coffee," I said with a nod at the table. "And Teddy will cook you whatever you want," I went on, then added with a grin, "if we have it."

He sat down on one of the boxes and reached for a cup.

"Sugar? Milk?" Teddy asked.

"I drink it black," he replied and took a sip. "It's good," he sighed.

After he had eaten the steak he had wished for, he got up and left the tent. A few minutes later he was back with his sleeping bag and a small tarpaulin.

"I sleep on the floor," he said, curtly, and without waiting for my approval, pushed the three boxes to one side, spread the tarpaulin and rolled out the sleeping bag. Then he disrobed and slipped into the bag. Moments later he was asleep.

He's obviously pooped. But that's no reason to be rude, I thought annoyed. Not being sleepy myself, I began to read.

It was near noon when the Shooting Crew arrived in two large, tracked vehicles, each pulling a big sled loaded with supplies. Large floatation tanks were mounted above the tracks. That gave the vehicles an odd-looking shape. A fold-out trailer was mounted on one unit, whereas the other was equipped with a stake body containing additional supplies.

It was an efficient and well organized crew. Immediately upon arriving, each member bent to a different task, and within short time their camp was set up.

One of the fellows approached me.

"I'm Norman ... and boss of this outfit," he introduced himself. He had a deep voice.

We shook hands. "I heard of you," he said.

I smiled, but did not reply.

About my age, he was an inch or two taller than I. Although his lean face was partly frostbitten, it showed that he was in the habit of shaving. His movements were quick, his bearing commanded respect.

We exchanged a few words about the weather, the surface of the ice and the pending work program.

His eyes, a washed brown, roved over my camp and recording spread. He gave a nod in direction where George was working on the radio antenna.

"Has he found a problem with your way of doing things?" he asked, emphasizing, problem.

I scrutinized him. "Sort of," I said. "He's not happy with the way I set up the antenna. Said: I messed it up. He's fiddling around with it now."

"You got that right," he said and, for an instant, laid his left on my shoulder. "We'll talk later. Come and see us tonight," he added, then left.

I wonder how he gets along with George, I thought while I walked down the recording line, checking it for possible damages done by wind or animals.

On my way back to camp I saw that Norman had set up a theodolite, its telescope trained on the sun.

I approached him. In his left hand he held a stop-watch, and he listened to the time signal that was barely audible through the crackling of static noise a small, battery-powered radio emitted.

"Missed it!" he rapped, stooped and tuned the radio anew.

"You're also the surveyor, right?" I asked.

He straightened up. "Yes. But tell me how you

50

figured the bearing of your recording spread?"

I hesitated. "Why? Is it wrong?"

"No. The contrary. Hold it! Here it comes!"

There sounded the beeps of the time signal, loud and clear this time. I waited till he had entered his observation into his motebook, then asked: "How many times do you check it?"

He seemed surprised. "You know about these things?"

I nodded.

"No kidding?"

"Why should I kid?"

He smiled. "And George said ... but never you mind what he said. I'm still wondering how you did it. I mean the figuring of the bearing. With a sextant?"

"I have no sextant. I set a pole and used its projected shadow," I said and watched with satisfaction the astonished expression that came to his face.

"Thinking of it, it's really quite simple," he reflected. "And accurate," he added.

There was nothing I wanted to add, and so I left him to do his observation of the sun's altitude and figure out the longitude and latitude we were at.

George was tuning the radio when I entered the tent. He told me that he had lengthened, then shortened the antenna.

"But it was a tuned antenna," I remarked.

"Fiddlestick! Just listen," he said and raised Seismic 1 and Seismic 2.

"There! It's much better now!" he triumphed, signing off his transmission.

I thought the reception rather worse than before, but did not want to argue about it.

After a cup of tea I left to visit the Shooting Crew. As I climbed the few steps leading up to a vestibule of the fold-out trailer, the door flung open and I was greeted with: "Come in, come in!"

"I'm Leon," a dark-haired, round-faced fellow said with a strong French accent, and proffered his hand.

We shook. He was about five and one half foot tall. I reckoned that he was in his late twenties.

He pointed. "And this is Edgar," he said.

Edgar nodded. His Eskimo face was all smiles and his jet eyes glistened behind their narrow slits.

"We know who you are," Leon went on before I could introduce myself.

"Sit down and have a coffee," invited Edgar. "I'm from Tuktuyaktuk where I worked for Northern Transportation for twenty odd years," he added.

That's why he speaks English so well, I thought.

"Hey. Ekaksak, come and say hello!" he called to a young fellow who stood at the cooking stove. Then he turned to me again. "He's my son's son. He's only fifteen and don't speak much English."

"He will when I'm through with him," Leon kidded and grinned.

"French, you mean," Edgar jeered, then called: Ekaksak! Is that coffee ready?"

"Krilammi," the youth answered.

"No! No! That's soon!" Leon cried.

Ekaksak glanced at me, then said, haltingly: "Leon ... him ... my friend ... but nag-nag."

"Sacrebleu! I get you for this," Leon funned, took a duffle sock from the clothesline that span across the room, and threw it at the boy who caught it and put it on a chair.

He smiled. "You ... bad," he said and set the coffee pot on the table.

Norman entered. "Damn nippy," he said, breathing in his cupped hands, then rubbing them. He sat down. "Where's Mike?" he asked.

"Must be sleeping in the tent. Said, he was very tired," Leon explained.

"No wonder," returned Norman, and turning to me, added: "He worked all last night. Repaired the engine of our generator."

From the ensuing talk I gathered that Mike was not a mechanic, but a surveyor with a knack for solving mechanical problems.

"He's very good with engines and that sort of things," Norman said to me.

53

I also found out that Leon was what is called in
seismic operation, the Shooter, and Edgar, the
Shooter's Helper; that Ekaksak was cook and flunky
for the party; that Leon and Edgar would leave early
in the morning to drive back several miles whence
they had come, drill a hole through the ice, lower
two-thousand pounds of explosives to the bottom of
the Channel, and explode it as soon as the three
seismic recording stations were ready to record the
shot; that Mike and Norman would survey the shot hole
location; and that an aircraft would bring more explosives.

It was to be a busy day for everyone involved. I
liked the prospect and was looking forward with interest to start recording and checking seismic data
and plotting the results.

All things worked out as planned. The shot was
exploded and its seismic waves recorded by Tony, Bill
and myself. Dale brought the explosives, and Norman
and Mike surveyed and carried forward the traverse.

But what made that day even more memorable for me
were the things that happened unexpectedly and had
nothing to do with seismic work.

Dale, when circling our camp before landing the
aircraft, had spotted four caribou feeding on the
other side of the island.

"They're almost pure white," he reported.

I had read about this species and knew that they were Peary caribou, which are smaller than their relatives to the south, the barren ground caribou.

Ekaksak overheard Dale's comment. He exchanged a few words in their tongue with Edgar, then left for the trailer.

"He wants to shoot one of these caribou. It will be his first," Edgar explained.

His first or not, I wish I could prevent it, I thought, but did not say so because I had no right to interfere.

Minutes later I saw the boy leave camp. Over the creamy duffle shirt he usually wore he had slipped a dark-blue anorak of which the sleeves and hem were adorned with broad, colored ribbons. And he had a Lee Enfield 303 rifle slung over his shoulder.

Since my work for the day was done, and I was curious of how he was going to stalk the caribou, I followed him at a distance.

He did not have to stalk them, for they were more curious than afraid of him and did not run away. He closed in on them and at a distance of about fifty yards dropped to one knee, took aim and made a clean kill with one shot. The three remaining animals milled shortly, sniffed their dead mate, startled, turned around and trotted away.

He packed his bounty back to camp where Edgar gutted and skinned it and then cut up the carcass. He gave me a hindquarter which I put into our meat box. A few days later Teddy cooked some of the meat. But it was tough and we left the rest for the foxes.

Later in the afternoon I ran into Mike.

"I was looking forward to meet you," I said in the way of introduction.

"So was I," he returned with a twinkle in his blue eyes.

He was almost of my height and was clothed in arctic wear of the same sort I wore. His cheeks and nose were spotted dark, reminding of frost bite. He seemed a pleasant sort, and we hit it off all right and for a while talked about the work we did.

The caribou was not the only animal that got killed that day. As I patrolled the camp before turning in for the night, I heard a muffled explosion followed by crunching steps that became faint, then gradually strong again. Through the bluish veil of twilight came Edgar, rifle in one hand and with the other dragging a lifeless, furry creature.

"It's a big wolf. I killed him with one shot," he said with pride in his voice.

Instant anger rose in me. "Why the hell did you have to do that?" I burst out.

The smile on his lips vanished, and I knew that I had hurt his feelings.

The heck with it. I'm not going to apologize, I

told myself.

"He will make a large, soft pelt ... good to sleep on," he said at length.

It was a statement that surprised me because no one in our camps needed a wolf pelt to sleep on, for we all were equipped with down-filled sleeping bags. And I knew that he slept in the trailer where it was warm and cosy.

Then why kill such marvellous animal? I thought and wanted to ask him, but before I could do that, he said: "I haven't killed a wolf since I was in my teens ... and never one as big and all white as this one."

He told me then that the wolf had followed their train for many days; that he repeatedly had tried to shoot it, but always missed.

"He must have been really hungry because he came to the bait right away once he got its scent," he reflected, stroking the thick pelt of the dead creature.

He stretched it out on the snow.

"See ... the caribou gut worked well," he said to Ekaksak who had joined us and admiringly looked at him and the wolf.

I could neither value Edgar's pride nor understand why he had killed the wolf. But Ekaksak seemed to comprehend it.

We recorded three more seismic shots with varying amounts of explosives. After that was done the

Shooting Crew left and a few hours later, George. He
drove an early model snowmobile called 'Autoboggan'.
He had no tent for protection against bad weather,
just his sleeping bag and a small tarpaulin. Together with his rifle he had tied them onto a Nansen sled
which he pulled with the snowmobile. Five gallons of
gasoline and one quart of oil were his spare supply
of fuel. In a pocket of his parka he carried a screw-
driver, a pair of pliers and a small adjustable wrench.
How much ammunition for his rifle he had on him I did
not know. A small, battery-powered radio he used for
communication. A sandwich or two he carried under his
parka close to his body, and also a small can of orange juice.

When I mentioned to him the possibility of mechanical breakdown or becoming lost or meet with a serious
accident, he got angry and snapped: "Don't teach me!
I know what I'm doing! Not like you who almost got
crushed by a pressure ridge."

"That's a cheap shot ... and you know it," I objected.

"Cheap shot or not ... it's a fact," he returned,
mounted the snowmobile and drove away.

"Does that bolster your ego?" I shouted and followed him with my eyes until he faded from sight and
earshot.

Teddy and I retrieved the geophones and rolled up

the recording cable. This time we did not carry these items, but loaded them onto a toboggan Norman had left for us.

"I'll take yours when at Bill's camp," he had said.

"Much easy now," Teddy remarked as we strained on the towropes.

I agreed, silently, but was still gasping.

CHAPTER 3

My next recording station was to be near Table Island in Belcher Channel. To get there meant to travel north along the westcoast of Devon Island to Bill's camp, cross Prince Alfred Bay to reach the low land beneath the Douro Range, then over land and a chain of lakes to Arthur Fiord and, hugging the northern coast of Grinnell Peninsula, past Tony's camp to Cape Ogle. From there an eight-mile trek across ice to Cape Ursula, its bold bluffs the southern extremities of Table Island. It would be a journey of more than one hundred and twenty miles, I figured.

Having read accounts of explorers, I had a slight knowledge of how far a man could travel by dogsled in a day, and I put it at thirty miles. Therefore, it would take us four days, not counting the days lost to possible bad weather, rough ice, detours around stretches of open water, and many hazards I did not know yet. And I doubted that Andrew's team of dogs could pull a sled loaded with almost fifteen hundred pounds of gear.

"I want you there and ready to record in four days," George had said.

Although I would have preferred to travel by dogsled, I knew that it would not get me there on time. Furthermore, the Eskimo's arrival was overdue by

several days. Pondering his whereabout, I walked up
to the island's top and scanned with my fieldglass
the vastness of Wellington Channel until my fingers
were stiff with cold and shivers raked me, making it
impossible to hold the glass steady. I ran back to
camp. But Andrew's whereabout kept troubling my mind,
and when twilight fell I had been at the top of the
island several times more without having detected any
moving object on the ice or heard sounds that would
have heralded the arrival of the missing.

I could not wait any longer and decided to move
our stuff by aircraft. I raised Seismic 2 on the
radio.

"Send M-E-S or whichever aircraft is free to come
and pick us up, — over," I requested.

"Will do, — standing by," Bill replied.

Next day fog lay over the surroundings so thick
that we could not see anything beyond fifty feet.
Like silent, veiled ghosts it wafted across the ice
and adorned all things with the limitless splendor of
hoarfrost.

During the following night the silence broke. The
guyropes and wires began to hum and shake off the
frosty trimmings — wind bearing from the west chased
the fog. And when the sun rose, the sky was blue and
not a shred of fog lay over land and ice.

Hours later I sat in the co-pilot's seat and looked

down at the only stretch of seemingly flat, snow-
covered ice among the great jumble that lay off the
westcoast of Table Island. Dale pointed — I nodded.
He leveled the wings, let the flaps out, throttled
the engine, shouted: "Hang on! It will be rough!"
and nosed the aircraft downward.

Scared, my heart pounding, my body rigid, I stared
at the fast approaching surface, felt doomed, fancied
bits and pieces of the aircraft strewn all over the
crash site, and thought that it was lunacy to attempt
a landing at such a location.

The skis made contact, there were knocks, several
bounces, swaying motion, the tail dropped down, its
wheel rumbled, the aircraft slowed and glided to a
halt. I felt relieved and at once cowardly.

"I don't like such landings. They scare me," Dale
remarked, flicking switches.

He too? I thought and did not feel cowardly anymore.

He tapped the temperature gauge. "It's thirty-two
below. I'll put the engine cover on. You may as
well start throwing off your stuff," he said.

I did exactly that.

"I'll be back with Teddy and the rest of your gear
in four hours," he said, then added with a smile: "I
expect you'll have coffee ready by then."

A short time later he took to the air again. I

looked at my watch. It was two hours to midnight. The sun had just set. The yellow afterglow faded on the slopes of the island.

While we had circled in search of a suitable landing site I had seen a bear with two cubs at a hole in the ice where the snow was much trampled and splattered red. Motherbear had provided luncheon.

Although I was looking forward to meet polar bears in the wild, free and not behind bars or a moat, I felt apprehension about their present proximity. Their zigzagging spoors had led to within less than half a mile to where I stood now.

They've just eaten, and for all I know, it was a seal, which, I hope, they prefer to human. I'm sure they'll pass me up, I appeased my uneasiness.

Do you really believe that? my inner voice asked.

"No!" I said out loud, took the rifle from its cover and slammed a cartridge home. Then I began to sort out the equipment and to pitch the tent. But my uneasiness persisted and, once in a while, I paused in my activity, listened intently and scanned with my eyes the surroundings unsure of what to expect.

When Dale and Teddy arrived, not four, but six hours later, I had pitched the tent, heated it , and the coffee was ready.

"Had to land at Tony's place to refuel," Dale explained as I pointed at my watch and remarked that it kept accurate time.

I gave him a letter to mail at Resolute.

"A love letter?" he teased, and without looking at
the address, pushed it into the breast pocket of his
parka.

"Uh-huh."

"To one of your girl friends?"

"No. To my wife."

"Your wife?" he blurted out.

I smiled. "Does that surprise you?"

He hesitated for a moment. "Somehow it does. You
know ... leave your family all alone for such long
time and expose yourself to all these dangers."

"We have no children."

"That's different, I guess."

"Not really," I said.

That seemed to puzzle him, but ended our conversation. Shortly after, Teddy and I watched him take
off and slowly vanish from sight.

During the following day and night Teddy and I
labored with only short breaks for meals and the occasional 'warming-up'. We laid out the recording
cable, planted and hooked up the geophones, set up
the instruments and the radio antenna masts, strung
the antennae and tested the system for flawless recording. We also rolled drums with fuel, dragged and
heaved crates and boxes of explosives, all of which

was for the Shooting Crew, for George had decided to
stockpile these items at our camp. It took three
airplane loads to bring them from Resolute. With the
third George arrived. He told me that he had considered my request for a snowmobile and sled and that I
would get both within the next few days. Then he in-
spected my setup and found it to be in order. Before
he boarded the aircraft he reminded me that I was
still green in this country and that he would keep
close watch on my performance.

"Big Brother, right?" I taunted.

Whether it was wrath or delight that reddened his
stubbled cheeks, I did not know. I saw his lips move,
but for the roar of the engine I could not make out
what he said. I doubted, however, that it was a bles-
sing because he did not return my good-bye waving.

I had forgotten all about bears and was heading
back to camp after a walk along the mile of recording
spread when, suddenly, a large bear ambled out of the
nearby ice pack. There it stood, less than the
length of a football field distant, and sniffed and
padded the snow. My heart leapt in terror. I froze
in my tracks and I hardly dared to breath. My mind
reeled and frantically tried to figure the chances I
had, for I had left the rifle in the tent.

Run? ... Perhaps! But not before he shows signs
that he has winded me. What else? ... Pray? Wouldn't

help ... or would it? You belong to the wrong sort
of guys, my inner voice insisted, and I could see
with my mind's eye how Satan gloated and rubbed his
hands.

Then that's it! I silently cried. Not necessar-
ily, a faint heartening whispered, and my natural
curiosity grew. I began to feel thrilled while realizing that I was in mortal danger.

Though evening ten o'clock, it was still light,
and I could clearly see the yellow tint in the bear's
long, white fur. It was a male, I was sure of that,
for no cubs had appeared on the scene. He stood
about four feet at the shoulder, and I guessed his
length to be six feet, if not more.

He lifted his head and swung it from side to
side — sampling my scent, flashed in my mind. Then
he sniffed the snow and began to advance in my direction.

"He's scented me!" I almost shouted, gulped
frightened and decided to run. But I hesitated for
the moment, and that saved me from getting killed or
severely mauled, for the bear stopped after a few
steps and stuck his nose into the snow.

He veered around, stuck his nose into the snow
again, walked a few steps to repeat the same. And
then he rose on his hindfeet and with his frontlegs
held stiff, bounced once, twice, a third time, broke

through the hard-crusted surface and disappeared from sight.

Moments later he emerged with a limp, white, furry creature clammed between his jaws. What kind of animal it was I could not make out, neither did I want to know — my only concern was how to escape unharmed.

The bear shook himself. A shower of sparkling snow crystals flew from his coat that made it look as if he had been procured by the wand of a sorceress. Then he vanished into the ice pack.

I sighed with relief and resolutely decided to leave the scene. But anxiety returned. Peering warily from side to side through the increasing duskiness, I shuffled irresolutely toward the tent.

I told Teddy about the encounter. His face showed no emotion as he said: "Saw big bear. You go. Me think, why no gun?"

George's remark sprang to my mind. Yes, I'm still green in this country, I thought and promised myself never again to forget to pack the loaded rifle.

I recorded the weather, something I did three times daily. And then I began to read. But after a few pages I put the book aside. I could not concentrate on the story because it bothered me not to know what kind of animal the bear had caught and killed. Before long I decided to go and hunt for clues.

"Go kill bear?" Teddy asked as I checked my rifle

before leaving the tent.

"No. Go look what bear kill," I replied, falling again into his jargon, and realizing it, added: "Do you want to come along?"

He shook his head. "Me stay," he said and resumed whittling. He was making a sling shot from a piece of slat and rubber bands.

"For my little boy," he had explained a few days earlier.

The boy was three years old and father's pride, I gathered.

The tracks of the bear were still clearly visible. I climbed a large chunk of upheaved ice to make sure that no bear was near. Set at ease, I went to where the male bear had broken through the snow cover. Under about two feet of hard snow was a hollow the extent of which I did not see, and to climb down into it I did not dare. The floor of it was glazed and splattered with blood.

The puzzle remained, and not before I had followed the tracks for some distance into the jumble of ice pack and stumbled onto two small , furry flippers did I know the answer — the bear had added a seal pup to his diet.

Like any bear I had met before: grizzly, black or brown, he obviously had the same acute sense of smell and, thus, had detected the seal pup in its lair under the snow. Being a powerful carnivore, it had been easy for him to break into it, kill the pup and make off with it.

I had witnessed a seldom observed act in the realm of the great white bear.

(I had read that seal pups cannot dive for safety till they molt at an age of about one month because their natal coat would become waterlogged and they would drown).

"That the bear smelled the pup saved my life," I said to myself. Talking to myself is a habit I often fall into when I am alone.

Walking in a roundabout way back to camp, I came upon another bear's spoor that was almost obliterated by drifting snow. I reckoned it to be perhaps a day old.

Whenever I hit upon the spoor of an animal I feel in some strange way compelled to follow it, and so it happened now — I followed the bear's tracks. Its zigzag course appeared to me evidence of an aimless amble. But when I found the remains of a seal near a breathing hole, I immediately revised my conjecture — the bear had really hunted and not just ambled aimlessly about the ice pack.

What was left of the seal were bones neatly stripped of meat and hide. It was the work of arctic foxes whose paw prints dotted the snow all around.

Knowing that there would be leftovers, these cunning creatures had followed the bear. (The polar bear devours only a portion of the seal, preferably its blubber, the fatty tissue below the skin. The rest is welcome feed for the arctic fox. It is a rather strange association, bear and fox, but it lasts during the winter months and warrants the fox's survival).

Twilight faded when I returned to camp. I smelled the aroma of freshly made coffee. Teddy, busy with cooking, turned around.

"You not here ... me hungry ... cook food," he said.

Bacon sizzled in the frying pan and slow clucks came from the coffee percolator.

"Make bannock.... you like?" he went on, turning with a spatula a thick cake baking on the heated griddle.

"I sure do. Make plenty of 'em. I'm starved," I replied, put the rifle on my cot, shed mittens and parka, then sat down to breakfast.

The temperature had risen to a few degrees below zero. Low clouds covered the country and wind, blowing from the west, sprang up. We banked the tent high with snow and secured all stores left in the open.

By evening a storm raged and shrieked and great gusts cut visibility to almost zero. It lasted twenty hours and buried the boxes and crates under huge drifts. In its wake came fog and light snowfall that lasted half a day.

I inquired by radio when I could expect the next seismic shot.

"Not before tomorrow, — over," Tony transmitted.

I was glad because it gave me enough time to climb to the top of the island, something I had wanted to do since I had arrived at the present location.

The sky was cloudless, the sun a bright spot to the south. The temperature was still hovering around the zero mark on the Fahrenheit scale. It was ideal weather for climbing. And I took for granted that it would be an easy climb.

But it turned out otherwise. I floundered through huge snowdrifts, broke through crusted, waist-high snow, clambered over rocks and ridges, and climbed up ice-covered gullies and along narrow ledges where the footing was precarious. There were moments when my heart pounded and shudders ran down my back, and I doubted the sanity of my doing. But the lure of gaining height persisted and kept me climbing.

I reached the top unscathed. The view was immensely wide. The air was alive over the white landscape. Like a flame, it scintillated, mirrored and heightened all objects, and created mirages of deceiving shapes and sizes.

To the west loomed Exmouth Island. It resembled

an oceangoing vessel bound in a benumbed turmoil of
waves in whose wake lay Eskin Island looking like a
whale's back. The rest of Belcher Channel, its white
tinted blue, was covered with a mosaic of smooth and
rough ice.

Though this scenery was devoid of life and un-
touched by any kindness of nature, it held an attrac-
tion that bewitched me in spite of my realizing that
there was no pretense, only merciless reality; that
it revealed a truth that made me feel small, insig-
nificant, but also glad to experience all this, which
was far beyond of what I had expected to find.

Glassing with my binoculars the distant ice surface, I detected a line of dark dots. They were moving at what appeared snail's pace. Repeatedly checking the progress of these dots, I became convinced
that it was a team of dogs pulling a sled.

"It's Andrew!" I cried excited.

I figured it would take him several hours to reach
our camp, enough time for me to descend and to be
there on his arrival.

But I had figured wrongly, for the sun had traveled
a full day's orbit across the northern sky before he
arrived.

He seemed weary, the dogs fagged. The sled was
loaded with a blue-painted box, frozen chunks of meat,
polar bear skins, their flesh side turned out. A

tarpaulin and a tent lay on top, and all was lashed down with thongs. Under one of the thongs stuck a rifle.

"Nanuk," he said with a smile and pointed at the skins. "One ... big," he went on, stooped slightly and showed with his mittened right a height of about two feet. "Two," he said.

A mother bear with two cubs! The ones I've seen from the air! shot through my head. I felt regret, but anger, too.

"Where?" I demanded with a sweep of my right.

He pointed whence he had come. "Ublumi."

"Ublumi?" I repeated, puzzled.

"Ima," he said and nodded, vigorously.

This did not help me to understand what he meant. "What's ublumi?" I asked.

His smile widened. "Ima, ima."

"No, no," I insisted. "Me," I tapped my chest, "not ... know ... ublumi," I said, pronouncing each word, slowly.

For a moment he seemed perplexed, then he smiled again. "Ublumi ... todi," he emphasized.

It was I who was perplexed now. Todi? Todi? I tried in my mind. "Ah ... today!" I exclaimed.

He nodded emphatically. "Nâmaktok," he gutturalized.

I did not asked what nâmaktok meant, but thought

that there would be enough time to find out. Being
at a loss what to do or what to say next, I grew increasingly embarrassed. I raked my head for an appropriate excuse to break the silence and to get a
reason to leave as he made a sweep with his hand
across his dogs and sled, then pointed downward and
said: "Okay?"

"Yes, yes! Certainly! Very good!" I exclaimed
without a moment's hesitation, and hoped that I had
interpreted his gesture correctly — that he wanted
to pitch camp where he stood. It was about fifty
paces from our tent and out of the way of the recording spread.

"Nåmaktok," he said and walked to the dogs.

He's said it again ... that nåmaktok, I thought
and tried to pronounce it the way he had gutturalized
it. I did not know yet that I had said the same in
English just a moment before: very good. I found it
out later when we became better acquainted and began
to teach each other in our respective tongues.

(Nåmaktok can also mean: it is good).

Teddy had not joined us, but watched and listened.
He stepped beside me now.

"Good dogs," he remarked.

This induced me to look more closely at them.
They were huskies of almost identical size. Their
color, however, ranged from jet to buff with white

and cream mixed in. They wore harness made of strong
canvas, and each was tied to a single trace leading
to the sled. Some of the traces were tangled. Why
that was, I had no clue. The dogs lay on the snow
and faced Andrew, their master.

"Him say: nanuk. My people say: wabask. You say:
white bear," Teddy interrupted my observing the dogs.
"Much different," he added after a pause.

"You're right," I said. "But we say: polar bear
and not white bear."

He looked at me with a face that was utterly impas-
sive and did not reveal what he thought. By now I
was used to that conversations with him were a matter
of long, pregnant, as if deeply thought over pauses
before he phrased the answer or question. Seldom did
he express spontaneously his knowledge, and never his
feelings. He was in this no different from other
Indians I had met and from whose verbal exchange I
had learned that they are masters in the art of the
pause, giving thoughtful context to a discussion.
Therefore, I waited for him to reply, but was called
away by the radio's loud announcement: "Seismic 3 ...
are you ready to record, — over."

By the time I had recorded the shot, developed the
paper record and hung it up to dry, and was free to
go and watch Andrew secure his outfit, perhaps lend
him a hand, he had laid out a long steel chain,

anchored its ends in the ice, and tethered the dogs
to it. Presently, he was chopping up with an axe
flint-like chunks of bear. The dogs watched in eager
anticipation of getting their rations, strained
against their tethers and licked their chops. He
threw the pieces of meat their way, not randomly, but
in selected order. Observing it, I remembered what
Bruce, the R.C.M.P. officer at Pond Inlet, had told
me the previous year about the dog's hierarchical
standings.

"Thanks, Bruce," I muttered now, for I realized
that he had told me the truth — there was really a
top dog while the others had their ranks, each subordinate to the one above it.

Before a piece of meat, weighing about five pounds,
hit the snow, the recipient snatched it, snarled fe-
rociously, then slunk away as far as its tether would
allow. There, the brute lay down, pinned the meat
with its front paws to the surface and chewed on it
while warily watching its neighbors. Some dogs , apparently afraid that another could rob it of its
portion, tried to gulp it down in haste. But such
hard was the piece that the particular dog invariably
choked, disgorged it to try anew. Often, another
snatched it away or contested its ownership what re-
sulted in a furious gnashing of teeth.

The feeding was an act of ferocity. Each dog

was willing to fight for even the smallest morsel, and several times Andrew was forced to stop chopping and to part two combatants before they injured each other seriously. He pounded them with the axe handle. The dogs cringed and cried under the blows, but did not let go of each other until they received forceful kicks, too. Feeding over, they seemed to lose interest in each other, yawned and stretched themselves, urinated or defecated, and after a while lay down and curled up, their snouts buried in their thick fur.

Having cared for the dogs, Andrew unloaded the sled and turned it over. He checked the gliding surface of the wooden runners which he had coated with ice and polished to a smooth, rounded shape. The ice was chipped in places.

On a one-burner stove he made tea, drank a cupful, dark and without sugar, then scooped snow into the remaining tea until it formed slush. He applied the slush to the chipped portions of the runners and carefully polished it with his mittens to a hard, glossy surface.

After he had pitched his tent, put his sleeping bag and a few other items inside it, he looked over the dogs, urinated, than crawled into the tent. All these things he did without uttering a word or taking a rest or giving Teddy and me a sign that he expected us to help. It was evident that he was used to do it alone.

Nothing more to watch, Teddy and I left for our tent to have a meal. He cooked for three persons, then went to invite Andrew, but returned alone.

"Him, sleep," he said, handing me a bowlful of French onion soup.

Before I turned in I made the round of our combined camps. Some dogs lifted their heads and sniffed my scent which was familiar to them now. None did more, and after a few moments of watching me with blinking eyes, stuck their snouts into their fur again.

From a distance, faint and far, came the mournful callings of their wild relatives, the wolves. Only the twitching of ears showed me that the dogs heard it, but were oblivious to it.

It was different with me. A slight shiver ran down my back and a great longing rose in me to share these moments with Nelly who also likes to hear the wolves. I felt lonely and sentimental. I left for the tent and began to write a letter to her.

Hours later I was awakened by rustling, growling, low and sporadic, and also the sounds of gulping.

Bear! I thought alarmed.

"Nonsense. The dogs would be in an uproar," I said half aloud, got up and dressed myself.

Teddy was asleep. He did not stir, and I was

amazed that the ongoing commotion did not wake him.

Peeping through the tent flaps, I saw two dogs
with their heads in our meat box. I rushed at them,
shouting and waving my arms. One ran away, the other
thrust his wolf-like head at me, the slaver dripping
from his ivory fangs, growled menacingly and then,
unsure of my reaction, lowered his head and groveled
backward. I gave him a kick — he snapped. I gave
him a second kick, this time as forceful as if I intended to send the oval ball flying between the up-
rights at the stadium. He yelped, turned around and
ran after his mate. I felt relieved because I did
not know wheter he would have attacked if pressed
hard.

The two marauders had freed themselves from their
tethers, had sniffed out our meat box and devoured
most of the frozen pork chops and frankfurters. I
was furious. Then I remembered George's prediction
that I would be sick of dogs at the end of the survey.
Now I wondered about its possibility. It was only
the second day we had dogs in camp, and two had raided our supply of meat. What would be next?

Since Teddy and I had moved from Seal Island to
the present location by aircraft and not as previ-
ously planned by dogsled, we had overtaken the
Shooting Crew. Now, after two uneventful days during which the weather had remained pleasantly mild

and no dog had broken its tether to rob our supplies
and bears had stayed out of sight, the Shooting Crew
caught up with us.

It was late afternoon when they arrived. They did
not cheer, but looked exhausted, and after they had
pitched their camp we did not hear or see any of them
for almost eight hours.

During these hours the weather changed — a storm
began to blow. It halted all work and confined everyone to his quarter. Yet after a while, to escape
boredom — a thing that ails most individuals left
without habitual work — one by one congregated in our
tent which, within short time, became a sort of gambling saloon. Leon, Edgar, Mike, Ekaksak and Teddy
tried their luck in a game of five-card stud. They
draped with a red blanket the box we used as table.
Their dreary moods changed to cheerful disposition.
The bets were laid — there was an occasional sigh,
the odd curse, a short laugh, a whistle — nickles and
dimes changed hands.

Norman and I stood with cup in hand, our backs
warmed by the space heater, and loosely watched the
game.

"There were moments when I thought we'd had it,"
he said and took a sip of coffee.

I gathered that he was referring to their
encounter with the pack ice that lay between Grinnell

Peninsula and Table Island, and which they had crossed to reach our camp. I had observed that he had not shaved, that his cheeks and chin were stubbly and showed recent frostbite. But it was not his looks that drew my attention, it was the matter-of-fact tone of voice in which he spoke. It sounded final, without emotion.

"Was it that bad?" I asked.

I remembered that I had felt great anxiety when I had seen that mass of jumbled ice and had pictured myself crossing it on foot or with a team of dogs.

"Merde! I almost wet my pants at times," Leon remarked. He had overheard our verbal exchange.

"Sacrebleu! I better watch what's going on here or I'll lose my shirt!" he exclaimed, looked at the cards in his hand, then at his opponents, one by one, then at his cards again.

"I'll match that," he decided and tossed a dime to where several coins lay on the blanket.

"I knew that pack ice was ahead. Dale had told me so," Norman went on. "But never, never have I seen such mess before. It looked as if a huge sea creature had run amok, ripped the ice to pieces and splattered it all over hell. Some chunks were the size of houses, some were glare ice, and some were covered with hard-crusted snow. There were huge drifts, hard on one side, soft on the other. There were cracks.

They scared me most. One never knew where they were under all that snow, and how wide they were." He took a deep breath. "I tell you ... and I really mean it ... I never want to experience something like that again. I think it was just ignorance and a large dose of luck that we made it without losing equipment and that no one got hurt."

A weary smile crossed his face and he seemed to fall into contemplation. I waited for him to continue.

"It sure was bad," he said at length. "It took us three days to cross these few miles. We broke a track on one unit. It had slipped sideways into a wide crack I had not seen. I was driving at that time. Boy, was I scared."

He took another sip of coffee, then told me more about their ordeal. It had taken them half a day to repair the track. Then they got stuck in deep snow, had to unload the supply sled, shove and push and winch over long distance to find hard surface again.

"And the worst was that we had to carry all that gear through that damned soft snow. We almost gave up. I felt it in me and saw it in the faces of the guys."

He looked at his crew who were oblivious to anything, except their game of cards.

"They're great guys. The best. But without Edgar,

I doubt that we could have made it. He's quite a guy.
He certainly knows his stuff ... I mean: how to get
through such a mess of piled up ice. After that soft
snow he walked ahead and showed us where to drive."

He emptied his cup.

"It's good coffee. Is there more of it?" he said
with a grin.

I took the coffee pot from the low burner of our
cooking stove and refilled our cups.

"Does anyone else want some?" I asked.

"I cover that and raise you a nickle," said Mike.

Norman laughed. "They're a bunch, aren't they?"

"So Edgar walked ahead," I encouraged him to continue with the story of their struggle.

"Right. It was scary just to watch him. Once he
sank up to his waist into slush and had a heck of a
time to get out of it."

"Slush?" I asked, surprised.

"Yes ... slush. The spot where he went through was
like a bowl in the middle of huge chunks of ice and,
I guess, water had seeped in through cracks."

"Did he not see it in time?"

"Apparently not. It doesn't show on the surface.
Anyhow, he got wet, but not just up to his waist ...
almost totally because he slipped and fell while trying to get out. I told him we would stop for him to
change into dry clothes. But he didn't want that.

He only changed his duffle socks, then kept going."

I could not refuse Edgar the tribute of a whistle.

"Wow! What a tough guy," I said in an undertone.

Whether it had been my whistle or what I had said, the guys halted gambling and stared at me for a few moments. Then they resumed betting.

"How old is he ?" I asked Norman.

"Forty-five, perhaps older," he returned. "But why don't you ask him."

"I certainly won't!" I blurted out, startling the guys again.

"Sorry," I apologized.

A chorused grumble was their reply.

"What else happened?" I asked Norman after a while.

"At times, it seemed to me that the pack was moving and we could really be in trouble. Not that I could see it move ... no ... but I felt it during the night when we rested. It sure scared me," he said and took a deep breath as if to free himself of an oppression.

"But that's nothing new for you, right?" he added.

I smiled. "So Bill told you about my experience at Seal Island."

"No, it was Dale. But why didn't you tell us?"

I shrugged my shoulder and said: "It happened and so what was the use talking about it."

"All alone and nobody to help? Weren't you scared?"

"You bet I was. But only till I saw what was happening. After that I had no time to be scared. I had to act ... and fast for all I knew."

"Why didn't you put everything on the island in the first place? It would have been safer."

"I know. But Dale couldn't land there."

He shook his head. "What a country! I think, we all must be crazy to be here."

"Perhaps," I said with a grin.

The storm was short-lived. By evening the wind had dropped, and the sun shone from a cloudless sky.

Everyone went back to work.

"Did you win or lose?" I asked Teddy when we tidied up our tent.

"Make much," he replied and showed me a handful of nickles and dimes. "Feel good," he added with a smile — a rare showing of his emotion.

"Have you seen Andrew?" I asked, changing the topic.

Andrew had eaten breakfast with us, then left and not returned since.

"Him sleep all time," Teddy replied.

"That's incredible. I couldn't sleep that long. I would ...,"

"This is M-E-S. How's your weather? Seismic 3," interrupted the radio's loudspeaker, and I could hear the droning of the aircraft's engine resound in the cockpit for a moment.

Before I could reply the droning noise came through
the loudspeaker again, and an instant later: "Did you
copy that? Seismic 3."

"Copy you strength five. Go ahead," I transmitted.

"Give me your weather, — over."

"Sky CAVU, wind calm, temperature plus five, barometer steady at three ... zero ... one ... fiver, —
over."

These were the data from my weather chart which I
had updated less than an hour earlier. (CAVU means:
clear and visibility unlimited).

"Got it. Will land at your place in forty-five
minutes, — over ."

"M-E-S, watch out for drifts, — over," I warned.

"Thanks, will do."

"Seismic 3 standing by," I transmitted, and when
the loudspeaker emitted two clicks, a signal that the
pilot had received my last message and had nothing
else to say, I hooked the microphone into its holder.

Dale landed the aircraft within the time he had
estimated.

"Here's mail for you and Teddy," he said and handed me a few letters.

I pushed them into my pocket, but not before a
glance had shown me on one Nelly's handwriting.

"Did you bring a snowmobile and sled?" I asked,
hiding my emotion. It was the first mail I received

since I had left home.

Dale opened the cargo door — and there they were.
I motioned to Teddy and Andrew to come and help unload. We were the only left in camp. Norman and
Mike were surveying line some miles west of the camp.
Leon, Edgar and Ekaksak had left with their vehicle
and supply sled to drill a few holes through the ice
and to lower explosives to the bottom of the channel.
All this was done in preparation for the next seismic
shot.

To unload the sled was easy; it was a 'Nansen' and
weighed little. The snowmobile, however, was unwieldy and just about all four men could handle. We
set up four fuel drums close to the cargo door, then
shoved the machine onto them , and from there to the
ground. Doing it that way prevented damaging the
fuselage.

Dale told me that he was going to move Bill and
his outfit to King Christian Island.

"I want to do it as long as the weather's good,"
he added, then climbed into the cockpit.

"Now don't forget to read the letters," he called
when he had started the engine and was running it up.

And that was what Teddy and I did.

Nelly's letter was three pages long. After I had
run my eyes down each page, I read them slowly, often
reading entire sentences twice. She wrote that she

was in good health, but was lonely — 'tu me manque' —
and that she was passing the time with working in the
garden, planting, but mostly weeding.

'I listen to the radio and hear what's happening
all over the world except where you are. And if I
should ask the radio man to tell me something about
what's happening where you are, he would say: how
should I know?

'And had we a telephone, and should it ring, I
would know in advance that it would not be you an-
swering my hello because where you're working there
are no telephones. It makes me sad to know that all
this is so.'

She also wrote that she wished she could be with
me regardless the physical hardship and dangers she
imagined to be many; that it was no good to be separated over long periods of time.

'I would be the happiest woman in the world should
you walk in through the door right now. I know that
this is impossible, but I also know that you will return as a man who followed his calling and is content
because of it. And this important for both of us.
Please, make time fly.'

"Oh, darling," I whispered, and my heart swelled
with love and longing.

I folded the letter and put it into my diary.
Then I looked at Teddy. He sat on his cot and stared

at the floor. The letter he had read he held in his hand.

"From your wife?" I asked.

He had told me that she was expecting again.

"Yes ... had child," he replied, curtly.

"Boy or girl?"

"Girl!" he burst out, stuck the letter in his pocket, stood up, took his 22-rifle from its cover, and left the tent without as much as a glance at me. I heard his steps fade with distance.

Hours later he returned with three ptarmigan he had shot and killed. These birds were still in their winter plumage — all white.

"Many around," he said and began to pluck them.

"Why in hell did you have to kill them?" I protested.

"Good in soup."

"That's not the point! We're not here to hunt!"

"Not hunt ... just walk around," he said.

Oh, what's the use, I thought frustrated, for I realized that he would not understand my aversion to what I considered senseless killing because we were not short of food.

For supper we had chicken noodle soup thickened with cut-up ptarmigan.

"You like?" he asked.

I nodded and so did Andrew who smacked his lips

and said: "Many good."

Teddy never talked about his wife and girl again.
It was as if he had forgotten them. And I never
asked him about the reason why, and was thus left
with the assumption that he was much disappointed
that his second child was a girl and not a boy as he
had apparently wished for.

Later that evening, when I walked along the recording line to check out a geophone that had shown
up dead on the instrument, I saw five wolves close to
camp. They sat apart from each other and watched the
goings-on. Their presence intrigued me. I slowly
approached the one nearest me and got to within perhaps thirty yards before he got up and sidled away a
few steps, hesitated, then took some steps more. I
burst into a short run; he veered round and fled,
stopped, faced me, cowered, ready to run again. I
backed up a few steps — he followed. I advanced — he
retreated.

The others had not moved, but watched with ears
cocked, their muzzles sampling the air. They seemed
alert, not frightened, rather curious. It struck me
that they had never smelled nor seen man and, therefore, did not know how dangerous he is.

They make easy targets for anyone who wants to
kill them, I thought.

"And such guys we have here," I said, half aloud.
I better drive 'em away before this happens, I went

on to myself, leveled the rifle and pulled the trigger. At the report all five fled short distance, sat
down again and kept watching me. The bullet had
struck the snow somewhere back of them. I had inten-
tionally aimed high. I leveled the rifle again. But
this time I took careful aim short of the one I had
run at. The bullet struck the ground inches away
from his front paws and spit snow mixed with dirt at
him. He jumped up, then fled over a rise of land,
the others after him. Shortly after I heard them
howl. It sounded as if they were accusing me of some
misdeed. The dogs in camp took up their strain and
for a while the air resounded with their lamentation.
I felt deeply moved.

As I returned to camp I saw that I had had spectators.

"You're a bad shot," Edgar said.

"I bet you'd miss a bison standing still at twenty
yards," Leon added, grinning.

"How will you defend yourself against a bear if
you have to?" Norman remarked, and I was not sure if
I had heard concern in his voice.

Only Mike said nothing. He looked at me with a
smile. I winked at him. His smile widened, and I
knew that he understood what I had done — scared away
the wolves.

I did not answer to the others' remarks, but

pretended shamefacedness. But silently I triumphed because I knew that no pelt could be collected this time.

Contrary to the assumption that pre-loading the shot points would facilitate and speedup the recording, it took all next day and most of the following night to record four shots.

Leon had detected strong current under the ice when he had pre-loaded the previous day. When he reported his observation it was accepted as a fact, and no one presumed that it could cause problems.

"That can't be five-hundred pounds. The signal is too weak," Tony commented by radio.

"You're right," Bill transmitted.

"But I loaded exactly five-hundred. So don't blame me, — over and standing by," Leon defended himself.

Had the current dragged away part of the charge? It was anybody's guess. My recording spread was relatively close to the shot. Therefore, I had set the instruments to suppress expected high signal amplitudes. The record I had received was good.

"I hate to lose that shot. So let's repeat it," Tony requested.

"Will do. But that cleans me out, — over," Leon informed.

"How long will it take you to reload?" Tony and Bill asked almost simultaneously.

"Don't know, — over and out," Leon replied.

And that was that.

Five hours later the loudspeaker boomed: "Sorry for the delay. Had to re-drill the hole," and after a pause: "Are you guys ready to record?"

"That's much better," Tony transmitted after the shot was exploded and he had seen the seismic waves on his monitor.   "How about you, Seismic 2 and 3?"

"It's good here," came Bill's answer.

"Mine's all right," I transmitted.

It had been the last shot for the location in hand. The Shooting Crew packed up and left. They drove westward, and within short time they disappeared over the horizon of the wide expanse of the frozen sea. It would take them a day, perhaps longer to reach the next shot point location. This meant time of rest for me and my crew of two, Teddy and Andrew.

"There's pack ice and open water farther west," Norman had told me after he had returned from the westernmost top of the island where he had erected a cairn, a marker for his line survey.

I did not worry about these condition, for I would follow their route. And where they get through we will, too, I thought with confidence.

Four hours after the Shooting Crew's departure Dale landed M-E-S, loaded with a 45-gallon barrel of gasoline and over twelve-hundred pounds of explosives, at our camp. George was along.

"When did they leave?" he demanded without greeting first.

"Hi," I said, ignoring his question.

"Cut that out!" he snapped.

I smiled. That seemed to rattle him. His imperious mien changed and he almost smiled, too.

"I guess, you're right. But I was upset that they left without waiting for us."

"Did they know that you were coming?"

He shrugged his shoulder. "I guess not."

I told him when they had left. He rushed into the tent, and seconds later I heard him raise the Shooting Crew on the radio.

Teddy, Andrew and I helped Dale unload the aircraft. After that, all of us had coffee. George was silent, pensive, then suddenly muttered: "How stupid. Now I have to bring it to them."

He got up. "Teddy, come along!" he ordered, then looked at me. "I'm taking your snowmobile," he added.

"And Teddy," I mocked.

He stared at me, and I stared back. His eyelids began to flicker. "If it's okay with you," he said.

"And if I would say, no?" I asked, faking seriousness.

"I would overrule you because I'm the boss," he

returned with a grin, then left the tent.

Teddy followed him.

"What a guy! You can't predict his moods," Dale remarked.

An hour or so later Andrew and I were alone. Dale was flying back to Isachsen, and George and Teddy were on their way with explosives for the Shooting Crew.

The weather was spring-like. The sun shone from a cloudless blue sky. The slow breeze did not stir the flags we had planted along the recording cable — they hung lifeless on their poles. And when I recorded the midday temperature, the mercury stood at two above zero on the Fahrenheit scale.

I decided to take a sponge bath and change into clean underwear. The used wear I soaked in the remaining bath water, then wrung them as best I could and dragged them on a rope over snow, a laundering method I had invented to save heating fuel. Frozen, but satisfactorily clean, I hung them to dry inside the tent.

I had begun pointing out objects to Andrew, say their names in English, and he, realizing my intention, said them in Eskimo. But most of the words he taught me I forgot within short time. Therefore, I tried another approach. I sketched the objects whose names in Eskimo I desired to know, and when

Andrew gutturalized them, I repeated them until I got
them right, often an effort that made him smile.
Then I wrote the word beside the respective sketch.
It gave me what I was looking for — a sort of picture
book dictionary. It also satisfied my desire to draw
things.

Andrew had an excellent memory, and hardly ever
did he forget the English word of an object I taught
him. He might mispronounce it, but that was all.

And now, after we had eaten the meal I had cooked —
chicken boiled in onion soup and cold leftover pancakes — I fetched my sketch book and we continued our
language lesson.

George and Teddy returned early in the morning.
Though he looked worn-out, George still snapped:
"Where in hell were you?"

"Why? What's up?" I asked, softly.

He stared at me for a moment, then said in a con-
ciliatory tone: "I tried to raise you on the radio,
but you gave no answer."

I had been out checking the recording spread in anticipation of the next shots to be recorded, and I
told him so.

"Oh, good," he sighed.

Had he worried about me not taking precautionary
measures without being told? Or had the physical
strain of the past hours made him cranky? Whatever

it was, at the moment he seemed satisfied with my performance and perhaps realized that I did not need con-
stant supervision — that I was a professional like
himself.

It was time for breakfast. I left the tent to
fetch a pailful of freshwater ice from the remaining
part of an iceberg Andrew had located and which, I
figured, had come from a glacier on Axel Heiberg Island. (Melting snow or sea-ice for making tea, coffee
or juice, gave them a salty taste).

When I returned Teddy and George were asleep. They
lay fully clothed, Teddy on his cot, George on mine.
Although I was hungry, I did not begin to cook, but
postponed it until the two had had their sleep. I was
afraid that the aroma of freshly made coffee and sizzling bacon would rouse them. I reckoned they needed
sleep more than food.

At six o'clock I passed on the weather report to
our base of operation at Isachsen. The sky was clear,
the temperature two above zero; the wind blew from
the east, its strength about ten miles per hour. The
barometric pressure had dropped slightly since midnight.

Then I raised the Shooting Crew.

"Yeah! What's up?" Edgar answered.

"When's the next shot?" I asked.

"Another hour. We're loading no. Be patient, —
over."

Three hours passed before Leon announced that they had drilled the hole; that the ice was thick, twenty-five feet, instead of the usual six to eight, and that they had lost two-hundred pounds of explosives down the hole, but were ready now to shoot.

"Seismic 3. If George is with you, tell him to bring more powder, — over," he added.

"Dammit! Can't these guys be more careful!" George exploded when I told him about the problem the Shooting Crew was having.

He and Teddy had slept to well past noon. In the meantime I had recorded two seismic shots. It were the last for my present location. Packing up and moving on was the next thing I had to do.

I planned to move my outfit in two sled-loads, one pulled by Andrew's ten huskies, the other by snowmobile driven by Teddy. I had gotten it down to brass tacks, and was convinced of its success. But Leon's request for more explosives altered this plan because George and Teddy, using the snowmobile and 'Nansen' sled, made another haul. The dogsled was now the only means of transportation I was left with.

CHAPTER 4

George promised that whatever supplies and gear I
had to leave behind I could recover by using the aircraft. And he advised me to take along only what he
termed : "essential things".

I used hand signs and some of the Eskimo words I
knew to explain to Andrew that we had to pack up and
head west. At first he appeared puzzled, but when I
repeated the signs and words with giving each empha-
sis, he grasped their meaning.

"Ima," he said, and I sighed with relief.

He piled onto the sled — kamotik, to both of us —
his blue box that contained spare thongs and several
harness for the dogs and some of his personal effects,
the bear skins and meat for the dogs. To these items
we added the minimum food and gear we would need for
our survival and to continue my work. The combined
load amounted to about nine-hundred pounds.

It was the first time now that I had a close look
at the sled. It was built of two twenty-six feet
long, thick, wooden runners to which traverse pieces,
measuring about three feet and resembling two-by-
fours, were lashed to their upper edge with thongs
cut from the hide of walrus. The entire construction
appeared to me flimsy and prone to fall apart. But
hours later I found that it really was a marvel of
design and construction, for though it creaked and

twisted, it withstood the punishing impacts the rough ice surface dealt it without falling apart or being damaged.

The rest of supplies and gear we piled up. I marked the location with a bamboo pole to which I tied colored ribbons and then stuck into an empty fuel barrel.

The wolves will get the meat and other foodstuff, I thought, and feeling bad about it, gestured to Andrew my intention to take all with us. He shook his head and resolutely tied down the load. I accepted his decision, for he was the one who knew how much the dogs could pull.

Then he hitched the dogs, each yelping and squirming with eager excitement, to the sled. Breaking it out with a hard jar sideways, he uttered: "Attai!"

The dogs hurled themselves into the traces, began to gallop fast and faster while the sled gained momentum. I ran beside it for a stretch, then followed Andrew's example and hoped on it, about three yards back of him.

The dogs followed the tracks left by the snowmobiles. After half a mile or so they stopped galloping and settled down to a steady trot.

My dream was fulfilled now — I sat on a sled pulled by huskies across the ice-covered arctic offshore. At that moment I was truly happy.

I watched the dogs how they strained in their harness and how they responded to Andrew's guttural chant
of orders. "Hoie!", they veered right. "Aghe!", they
bent left. "Attai!", they tightened the traces, their
backs arched up. It was a magnificent display of
man's mastery over the brute, its desire a chunk of
meat at the end of the day's toil.

Each dog was hitched to its own trace, ranging in
length from about twenty-five to more than thirty-five
feet. And since each dog chose his own route to pull,
the team formed thus a fan.

Table Island faded from sight, and a flat horizon
encircled us. The sky was a cloudless blue. I felt
the sun's warming rays on my parka, heard the high-
pitched squeal of the sled, both pleasant sensations,
and I almost succumbed to drowsiness while I gazed at
the scintillating white expanse or at the dogs who
shifted endlessly from left to right and vice versa,
hopping over or ducking under the other dogs' traces,
plaiting them gradually into one thick braid.

Andrew stopped the dogs and began to extract each
trace from the braid. It looked to me a hopeless
undertaking. But the traces, made of bearded seal
hide, were so stiff that they did not knot tightly
and, within short time, he had each dog tied to its
unraveled trace again.

On went the journey until the newly formed braid

prevented the beasts from pulling effectively, and
Andrew stopped them to unravel the traces again. This
process repeated itself at what appeared to me short
intervals, and every time it happened I expected
Andrew to curse or show signs of frustration. But he
remained calm, and that puzzled me. I was then still
too new in the arctic environment to understand that
such things do not matter; that the weather, the condition of man and beast and the terrain one meets are
more important than time; that they represent safety
or disaster. Its truth I was to learn shortly.

The first inkling that a change was imminent I got
when I saw thick fog lay over the ice ahead.

"There's pack ice and open water," Norman had told
me.

Pack ice we had met. Where possible, Andrew had
led the dogs around it. But where the ridges and
patches of crushed and tumbled ice had been long and
wide, and going around them would have taken us too
far from the tracks we were following, he had guided
the team in a masterly way through and over these obstacles, the sled twisting, sliding sideways and
slamming into chunks of broken ice.

Open water we had not encountered, and that made
me feel uneasy.

"Hey, Andrew!" I called and, not knowing the word
for fog in his tongue, pointed.

If I had expected to see any emotion in his face,
I was sorely mistaken, for it remained stoical.

Heck! As long as we're following the tracks we're
safe, I thought and relaxed.

Whether the fog had wafted closer or we had traveled into it, I could not say with certainty, for all
of a sudden the sun was plotted out, the air became
nippy, the surroundings featureless.

We were in whiteout!

All shapes of the surface, bumps and hollows, had
merged into a flattened, white background. I knew it
could spell disaster and the only safety was in waiting for the whiteout to lift or in shuffling along
the surface, alert to all kinds of perils hidden to
the eye. The dogs' instinct seemed to tell them the
same, for they advanced at a mere crawl, whining and
yelping in turns.

Andrew, leaning forward, peered straight ahead.
My feet began to freeze. I slid off the sled and
staggered alongside it until I felt warming circulation return to them. Then I hopped aboard again.

"Ho," Andrew uttered at length.

The dogs halted, turned to face him, then lay
down. What distance we had covered since the whiteout had begun I did not even try to guess.

He left the sled, shuffled a few yards past the
dogs, halted and swept with his right foot the snow-

covered ice. Then he bent down and seemed to examen the surface. I watched him with increasing curiosity, but remained on the sled.

He returned. "No innit," he said with a sweep of his left hand in direction we were heading.

Not knowing what 'innit' meant, I failed to catch the meaning of his gesture. A pang of frustration surged up in me. He sense it and smiled.

"Tumik," he said and pointed at his footprint, then at the tracks the sled had left. "Innit, innit," he repeated.

I understood. Tumik meant foot tracks, innit, tracks of the sled. My heart began to pound.

"No innit?" I croaked and pointed ahead.

He nodded. It meant we had lost the tracks we had been following, and I did not like the idea of it at all.

"Well, what on earth are we going to do now?" I asked, my voice still hoarse.

But as he nodded and smiled, for he had not understood a word of what I had said, I burst out in laughter. Here we were ... in whiteout and possibly near open water ... the latter being the reason for the fog, I assumed; had lost the tracks we ought to have followed, and had language lesson.

"It's lunacy!" I cried, and looking at him, saw that he did no more smile, but scrutinized me with obvious consternation.

Another bout of hilarity gripped me, and I burst
out: "Don't worry! I've not cracked up!"

Getting the drift of my outburst, he smiled again.
"Nâmaktok ... very good," he said.

I wanted to ask him what he thought our next move
should be, but I knew no Eskimo for: 'what do we do
next?' ... 'have you experienced this before?' ...
'what will happen?' ... 'is there grave danger or
not?'.

I felt helpless, and Arne's remark about possible
communication problems rose in my mind. Not so fast,
my friend, I thought, and out loud, said: "You ... me
... kringmerk ... kamotik ... stay here?" and pointed
down. (Kringmerk means dog).

He stared at me, and I hoped that he had perceived
the meaning of my words and gesture. After a few
seconds his face lit up and he nodded, vigorously.

"Ima," he said, took off his mittens, laid them on
the sled, reached up underneath his anorak and pro-
duced a small leather pouch from which he took a hand-
rolled cigarette. He lit it with a match and, seating
himself on the sled again, began to smoke.

I stomped my feet and threshed my arms for a while
before I climbed onto the sled, too. The dogs lay on
the ice, their muzzles covered with their bushy tails.

I had no idea of how long we waited. It seemed an

eternity. I did not think, I did not move. It was
as if I had become a part of the surroundings — benumbed. And so seemed Andrew to be a part of it.

Then a light breeze began to blow. It lifted the
fog, the whiteout diminished somewhat, the featureless surroundings took on shape again.

Andrew pointed. "Taku!" he said, calmly. It meant:
"Look!" There was no surprise in his voice — it
sounded matter-of-factly.

I peered into the still mist-veiled light, and
what I saw made my skin crawl and a chill tremor
seized my heart. There was water not more than hundred feet from where the dogs lay rolled up.

Good dogs. You sensed what was ahead, and that's
why you whined and crawled, I thought, and heaved a
deep breath.

Andrew shuffled past the dogs. I followed him and
almost caught up when he turned around and signaled
for me to halt.

"Sikku ... ice ... no good," he said, and holding
his mittened hands a few inches apart, indicated how
thick the ice was.

I shuddered.

It was no mere lead where the water showed, but an
expanse the size of which we could not see. Its surface was bluish-green and rippled in the breeze, and
haze lay over it.

I was scared and waited for Andrew to make the next move. I had to rely on his experience and trust his knowledge of the environment, something that made me feel utterly helpless. It was a humbling experience. for me!

After a few minutes we returned to the sled. He called the dogs' attention, grabbed the leader by its collar and led it at a right angle to the sled. The other dogs followed. The traces tightened, the beasts yelped, strained with their backs arched, their paws were scratching, digging, while he encouraged them with calm words. The sled scrapped sideways, piled up snow along its runners, and stuck fast. He did not have to point out the problem — I yanked and pushed, the sled broke loose, the dogs, yelping excitedly, hurled themselves forward, the sled shot ahead.

Andrew jumped onto it. I wanted to do the same, but slipped, lost balance, then sprawled on the ice. Before I could scramble to my feet the sled was beyond my reach. I cursed and ran after it.

Andrew had not seen me fall down — he urged on the dogs. The distance increased between us. I began to tire, tried to holler, but only a hoarse sound left my mouth — it did not carry far. I stumbled uncontrollably ahead for a while longer, then slowed to a shuffle.

Though we had turned away from the water, thoughts of thin ice and bears and of not catching up to the sled in time to be safe rose to my mind. But as sudden as they rose, as sudden I dismissed them. Shuffling ahead for some minutes, I recovered my strength and began to walk at a brisk pace.

Andrew and his outfit merged into a point. Yet that point remained in sight, began to grow larger, and then I saw him standing on top of the sled and looking my way. The dogs lay fanned-out on the ice.

"No look. Stop," he said as I drew close.

I knew that with "no look" he meant: "no see", but I did not correct him.

Tired I slumped onto the sled.

After he had smoked a cigarette and I was rested, we sledged on. The ice was smooth and rough in turns. Patches of fog wafted across it. They felt like cold, moist breath and made me shiver.

Andrew stopped the dogs a couple of times, stood up on the sled and peered ahead. I gathered that he was looking for something that was unknown to me. I did not ask what it was because I did not want to appear ignorant. All of a sudden, the dogs began to whine and to strain with eagerness at their traces. Had they smelled what Andrew was looking for — a bear?

I was not enthused about that possibility, for hunting bear was far from my mind. All I wanted was

to find the tracks we had lost, and to continue our
journey to my next recording site. To my relief, the
dogs' eagerness lasted only a few minutes, then they
settled to a steady trot again.

And then there was no shape to the ice — whiteout
had come back. We stopped and waited. I did not
know how far we had come and whether we traveled in
the right direction, for I was totally disoriented.
There were moments when I felt as if the surroundings
were grinning at me with sinister intent; that we
were trapped and had no way out; that we were to per-
ish. Looking at Andrew who seemed unconcerned, I
called myself fainthearted and tried not to think.
But as I heard the muffled sound of grinding and
shortly after felt a slight tilting motion, reminding me of what had happened at Seal Island, my mind
conjured up pictures of ultimate disaster.

The tilting motion continued for a few seconds.
Then a shudder ran through the ice and somewhere it
exploded with a loud noise. Then all was quiet again,
inducing an eerie feeling.

Minutes later the dogs got up, began to whine and
yelp, approached the sled and tried to climb it. We
fought them off with kicks and punches.

"Immerk," Andrew said and pointed to where the dogs
had lain. The snow seemed to flow away.

"Water," I breathed, shocked. "What are we going

to do?" I asked, putting some strength into my voice.

He nodded and smiled and then began to smoke. He had no clue of what I had asked.

He must have experienced this before, I thought, and though I did not enjoy the situation, anxiety left me and I became curious of what would happen next.

The dogs, possibly sensing that the water would not come closer, settled down, rolled up and stuck their muzzles into their fur.

After what seemed hours, a breeze picked up, the whiteout vanished and we could see the surrounding features again. And what a mess they were!

Straight ahead, in the direction we had been traveling, was ice piled high. It was perhaps the length of a football field from us, and I was sure that it had not been there before.

To our left, not more than thirty paces distant, the ice had separated and drifted, leaving an open, wide lead of which we saw neither its beginning nor its end. I kneaded a snowball and threw it into the lead. It hit the water with a splash. The dogs shot up and facing the lead, growled threateningly.

To our right, about a mile distant, there was a ridge of broken, tumbled ice that stretched on either side beyond the horizon. It had been there before — I was sure of that.

Back of us, the ice had remained flat, undisturbed.

Andrew pointed. "Go," he said, and lined up the dogs. That's the way we came, I thought while I strained to break out the sled.

It was perhaps an hour later when we hit an open lead. The ice was about five feet thick, and where it had ripped it was covered with a thick layer of frost. Thin pans of ice and lumps of slush floated in the water. It was too wide for us to cross .

Andrew pointed left, then right, and shrugged his shoulder. It meant: in which direction should we go.

How should I know? I thought, wagged my head, counted to seven for good luck, then pointed right.

He smiled, called: "Hoie!", the dogs veered right — we followed the lead in search of its end or a narrow where the dogs could jump it and we could shove the sled across.

The snow-covered ice stretched in waves before us. Coming into a trough of a long one, the sled tilted to the right, I felt a sharp tug, and off I was, sprawling on the ice. Scrambling to my feet, I broke through the surface and stood half-way up to my knees in slush. A few paces beyond me the sled rested on its crossbars. We were in a tidal pool. The dogs whined as if expressing sympathy for the mishap or that they could pull no more. But before long, one after the other lay down and rolled up. In spite of

being disenchanted with the whole affair, I chuckled —
what amazing beasts they are, I thought.

Andrew had not been thrown off, and I wondered if
he had anticipated such thing to happen and had been
prepared to reach for the sled's lashings in time. If
so, he could have warned me, I thought, irritated.

He pulled his harpoon from under the lashings and
slid off the sled. Sloshing in a zigzag course through
the icy slush, he tested the underlying ice with the
harpoon. At a distance of about sixty yards I saw him
climb out of the slush and, stepping in his soft-footed
manner, walk an additional stretch ahead.

Sitting on the sled and watching him how he did all
this with apparent calmness, ill-humor left me. I knew
that my feet were wet and freezing, but I did not feel
it — I only felt that they were numb. To change into
dry socks and duffels was useless because I had to get
into the slush again.

After Andrew had returned we unloaded the sled and,
sloshing back and forth, carried piece after piece of
the load to firm surface. Then, with the help of the
dogs, we moved the sled, yard by yard. It was hard
labor for us and the dogs.

Our mittens and footwear were soaked and frozen on
the outside, making them regular iceboxes. It took me
a long time to change into dry spares and to bring
back blood circulation to hands and feet.

Andrew did all this much faster, and when I had stowed the wet stuff and was ready to help him, he had loaded the sled and was lashing it.

He pointed at my feet and asked: "Okay?"

I nodded. "How about yours?" I asked, and realizing that he did not understand, pointed at his kamiks.

"Good ... much good," he said and smiled.

He unraveled the dogs' traces, and then we sledged on. We passed over a few more waves, their lengths getting short, their troughs less deep, and then the ice was level and smooth, making for easy traveling.

To keep from freezing, I rod and ran by turns. Andrew seemed impervious to freezing. He sat motionless on the sled while encouraging the dogs with his guttural chant.

Then fog engulfed us again. He stopped the dogs, and we waited. All of a sudden there was commotion. Tremors ran through the ice. I heard breaking, grinding, felt shifting, and a few seconds later I could feel that we were drifting. I was scared, but took heart as I saw that Andrew smoked, and none of the dogs showed fear or excitement.

While we kept drifting, I realized that I was most likely way behind scheduled time in arriving at my next recording site, and that it was perhaps questionable whether we would arrive there at all. Thinking of the latter, I felt doomed, but like before, gained confidence in Andrew's calmness.

It seemed hours before the fog lifted and we could see that we were near the edge of an ice floe that had broken away from the main ice sheet and was drifting with other floes in open water the extent of which we could not see. The floe we were on was about half of one acre in size. It moved rather fast, for the water swirled around it, giving me the idea that a tremendous current was at work.

(Years later when I worked in this part of the archipelago again, I arrived at the conclusion: though Belcher Channel freezes over, the ice cover is often thin, making it extremely treacherous to travel on it; that over large areas the ice cover is oftentimes ripped asunder by strong current, resulting in patches of open water and ice floes).

I had not the faintest notion of what would happen. But I hoped that the floe would close with the main sheet, giving us the chance to escape.

As if playing a game of tag, the floe drifted in and out, touched twice, however not long enough for us to cross over. Hours passed until it bumped with force into the main sheet and held fast.

"Attai!" Andrew called. The dogs hurled themselves forward while he and I shoved the sled onto solid ice. But there seemed to be no end to misfortune — we hit again a lead too wide for us to cross. Andrew said

a few words in his tongue, the meaning of which I
understood as he pointed downward — we would not follow the lead, but stay put.

Pointing to right and left, I asked: "Why not?"

He shook his head, and that was that. Is he waiting for the lead to close? I wondered, and decided
that this was a slim chance.

But it was exactly what happened after a time that
almost drove me to despair. Has he known it or just
chanced it? I asked myself, and my uneasiness increased, for I feared that there was far too little I
knew about the arctic environment and its whims to
allow me to get out of the mess we were in if I were
alone.

When the lead had narrowed to about six feet,
Andrew alerted the dogs who lay curled up on the ice
and were sleeping. Encouraged by his chant of orders
they lunged forward while I helped him to break out
the sled. The first dogs leapt across the lead. The
rest rushed after them. But one slipped and with a
terrified yelp landed in the water. To my surprise
the others stopped abruptly.

The unfortunate beast, whining softly, tried to
scramble out of the lead while its mates watched with
hairs bristling along their necks and backs.

Digging and scratching like mad, the trapped dog
drove its claws into the hoarfrost that covered the

sides of the lead. But underneath the layer of frost
was hard ice, and not before Andrew hauled on its
trace could it climb out of the lead. None the worse
for its unexpected bath, it only shook itself, pro-
ducing a fine spray of water that sparkled in the air.

"Attai! Attai!" Andrew urged. The traces tightened, the sled shot forward and across the lead. I
grabbed for it, missed, and almost ended up in the
water. He saw me blunder and slowed the dogs. I
caught up and swung myself onto the sled.

After some distance we met tracks made by machines.
A brisk wind dissolved the fog and I could see the sun
again. It showed me that we were heading west. The
tracks continued going straight except for where the
ice had cracked and shifted, sometimes to our right,
sometimes to our left. In some places the shift was
as much as perhaps one hundred feet. But the farther
west we traveled the less it became. I figured that
we were leaving the area of shifting ice cover, and
began to relax.

I did not know how long our ordeal had lasted, for
I had forgotten to rewind my watch, and the sun had
been plotted out.

It had been an unnerving affair for me. Andrew,
however, had not shown anxiety nor had he acted hast-
ily. I realized that traveling on the ice was to him
mere routine. This white expanse was to him not a

hostile environment as it was for me at that time; he traveled over it with inner tranquillity, taking the obstacles that barred his path as a matter of course, and was not upset nor bothered by them.

"That's the difference between him and me," I said, thinking aloud. I wonder if I can become this way, I went on to myself, and not having eaten anything since we had left Table Island, I felt suddenly very hungry.

"Andrew!" I called, determined to have a snack.

He turned his head, smiled and pointed in the direction we were sledging. Not more than one hundred yards distant stuck three bamboo poles in the ice. Their tips were tied together forming a tripod. And from each pole fluttered orange ribbons in the breeze. It was the marker Norman had left for me. We had arrived at my new recording location.

The site was deserted, and only much trampled snow let me assume that the Shooting Crew had used it as their campsite.

Andrew tethered and fed the dogs while I unloaded the sled, pitched the tents and prepared a meal. The sun was on the rise — it was breakfast time. But what I cooked was breakfast, lunch and supper combined into several huge servings. And then we sought the warmth of our sleeping bags.

CHAPTER 5

Although I had not slept in two days and as many
nights, I could not sleep, tossed restlessly for a
while, then got up and dressed. The weather had
closed in again. Low-lying clouds, driven by a brisk
wind, scudded across the ice, and snow drifted, slowly burying whatever supplies and gear I had left in
the open.

Andrew had retired to his own tent. I looked in
on him. He was asleep and I decided not to wake him,
knowing all to well that I deprived myself of his
help laying out the recording spread and setting up
the tall radio masts.

After erecting the masts, which proved a tricky
balancing affair in the prevailing breeze, I laid out
the recording cable. Having left the toboggan as a
nonessential item at Table Island, proved to have
been a wrong decision, for I had to carry the heavy
cable reels now. I staggered over hard-blown drifts,
floundered in deep, soft snow, and slithered over
patches of bare ice. The twenty-four geophones, each
weighing more than I cared for, I carried in pairs to
their respective hookups. It was strenuous work and
when, hours later, I staggered into camp I was worn
out.

The dogs lay at their tethers, apparently asleep.

But as I passed them all shot up into their tethers,
snarled menacingly with upper lips wrinkled, their
yellow fangs flashing, ready to attack. I froze in
my tracks and tried to figure the chances I had should
they do so. But when they caught my scent — I had
approached the camp upwind — they gave up their
threatening stance and one after the other returned to
its resting place where they curled up again. Though
they recognized me, none wagged its tail, and I knew
that they would never be friendly.

Andrew was still asleep. I cooked a meal and after
I had eaten it I set up the recording instruments,
tuned the radio, listened to the time signal and set
the watch. Then I transmitted that I was ready to record the next seismic shot.

"Good to hear you're all right. Was worried about
your whereabout," Tony transmitted in reply.

"Nice to have you back," Bill added over his radio.

"Thanks, guys. Does anyone know where George and
Teddy are? — over."

"This is the Shooting Crew. They left us a while
ago, heading your way, — over," Leon explained, and
after a few seconds added: "We're glad you're in one
piece, — over."

"Shooting Crew, are you ready to blast?" Tony asked.

"Yes. Just waited for Seismic 3, — over."

"Then let her go," Bill transmitted.

"Will do. Stand by," Leon replied, and shortly after, the loudspeaker emitted the blasting signal.

I counted to five, then pressed the recording button. Another secret of the Sverdrup Basin's sedimentation was recorded on strips of photosensitive paper. Two more shots I recorded before George and Teddy drove into camp.

"Where in hell were you?" George demanded, wiping the snow from his parka. "You're two days late!"

"I know," I replied, and in a few words told him the reason why this was.

He grew pale, and I did not get the dressing down I had expected. I was glad for that because I was very tired and not at all in a mood to argue or give lengthy explanations.

"I'm going to sack out now," I said, turned around and went into the tent.

He did not call me back.

I heard him talk to Teddy, start the snowmobile and drive away. I ran outside and called after him. But he was already out of earshot and shortly after disappeared over a huge snowdrift. He was heading for Table Island.

Teddy, still refueling his snowmobile, looked up and said: "Him hurry. Say, must follow. Go get powder."

I told him to bring me some food and the generator

I needed to charge the batteries with. "All of it is in the cache I left there," I explained.

"Me tell boss," he said, a faint smile on his lips.

"Aren't you hungry?" I asked.

He shook his head. "Had food in shoot camp," he replied, looked down the recording spread and up the radio masts, and I knew what he was thinking.

"I did it all alone," I said.

"Andrew ... no help?" he asked, and as I shook my head, I saw his eyes lose their stoic gaze and fill with embarrassment.

"Me cannot help ... must drive powder," he said.

It was one of the rare moments he let his feelings show. Unwittingly? I did not know.

"Me go now," he said, his face expressionless again.

"Be careful. There's open water and thin ice," I said.

He did not answer, but I gathered that he understood that Andrew and I had just gone through such condition, for he glanced at the dogs and the sled before he followed George.

A while later the wind died down and the sky cleared. The sun drew long shadows across the ice. The air temperature dropped rapidly from a pleasant ten degrees above zero to a chilling seven below.

I cooked another meal; this time for two. Yet as

I called Andrew that supper was ready, I received no
answer — he was still asleep. I ate my portion, set
his aside, washed the dishes, then bedded down to a
well-earned rest.

A dog began to howl and then each took up the
strain until the full-throated chorus swayed the air.
It was a woeful song that rose and fell in strength,
but seemed to hold the greatest secret of their race.
When it stopped I fell asleep to dream of wolf-like
creatures falling into wide leads, saliva dripping
from their fangs while scratching madly at the walls
of ice that kept them from getting at me. Several
times I woke to turn and to fall into the abyss of
another nightmare. In time, however, my sleep became
peaceful and when I awoke, six hours later, I felt
refreshed and was eager to experience another day in
this relentless arctic environment.

It was well into the afternoon before George and
Teddy returned from Table Island. They brought heavy
loads of explosives, but no food, no generator and no
gasoline.

"We had a hard enough time without having to haul
more weight," George replied as I accused him of leaving me in the lurch.

He described a scenery of pressure ridges, large
patches of broken, jumbled ice, of deep snowdrifts
where only flat surface had existed a few days earlier.

"No lead or open water?" I asked.

"Haven't seen any," he said, and I thought: how can that be? Andrew and I met plenty of them. Or has the ice shifted and closed them up?

Before I could remark upon this, he told me that he and Teddy would bring the explosives to the Shooting Crew.

"Then I'll send Andrew to get grub and the generator," I responded.

"No! You won't!" he snapped, caught himself, then added in a softer tone: "We had to leave several boxes of dynamite along the trail, and he must pick 'em up before they're drifted in and we can't find 'em anymore."

All my objections did not help to change his mind. I gave up and headed for the tent.

"I wouldn't mind having a coffee!" he called after me.

"You want it now or after you've told Andrew what he has to do?" I teased.

He grinned. "I like it after ... if you don't mind."

While we were having that coffee, I heard Andrew's chant of command, short yelps, and then the squealing of sled runners.

"How did you tell him? In Eskimo?" I asked, surprised.

"You'd like to know that, eh?"

I nodded.

"Then keep guessing," he said with a grin.

And I was none the wiser for it.

After he and Teddy had left I walked along the recording cable to check out a geophone that had shown up dead on the last record. I found the problem to be a loose contact, something that was more annoying than requiring much repair work.

Kneeling on the ice and hunched over, I caught a movement in the corner of one eye. Looking up, my heart gave a thud, my ears filled with the sound of the blood rushing through my veins, and a violent shiver ran up and down my back — not more than twenty paces distant stood a polar bear! It's a male, flashed through my head. His presence seemed so impossible, that I could hardly understand or accept it. But there he stood, sampling my scent, the scent of a creature he did not know and thus hesitated to rush at. The strongest and most ferocious animal of the Arctic had silently approached, and I knew that I had not much of a chance to escape. This made my blood run cold.

Though I felt utterly helpless, in my mind I tried frantically to master the situation. Should I yell or behave in a manner that might scare him, I asked myself. I did neither. And that, I'm sure, saved me

from being killed. (I did not know then that the
polar bear is highly unpredictable, will sometimes
scare easily, at other times not at all. Neither did
I know how lightning fast this carnivore can move).

Slightly heartened that he stayed put, I slowly,
carefully, reached for my rifle which lay beside me
on the ice. I must admit: I did not discover in me
the calmness and fearlessness many hunters are apt to
claim their trait. It was no physical exertion to
lift the rifle, but my heart pounded, my hand shook,
and perspiration wet my body. I raised it to my
shoulder and aimed at the bear while trying to remember if there was a cartridge in its chamber. I figured that I had only one chance: to flick the safety
and to pull the trigger, should the bear rush at me.

There was something ominous about that stand off,
and in inexplicable ways made me feel that the worst
was about to come. Desperation gripped me and I began to talk in a low, shaky tone.

"Please ... don't come any closer ... I'll kill
you ... should you do so ... go away and leave me
alone."

The prevailing cold numbed my feet and hands and
began to spread throughout my body. I began to shiver and thought of pulling the trigger to end the
nerve-racking situation, one way or the other when,
all of a sudden, the bear turned around and ambled
away.

"Keep on going and don't come back," I whispered.

I did not feel safer then because I was aware that he could turn around at any moment and I would face extreme danger again. To my relief he kept shuffling away from me. As he disappeared over a snowdrift I got up and headed for the tent, almost half a mile distant. Yet after a few steps, my nerves still tingling, I stood still, turned full circle while scanning anxiously with my eyes the immediate surroundings.

"Pull yourself together ... the bear has gone," I said out loud, and promised myself to return to camp without further delay.

Resolutely, I walked short distance, halted and turned in a circle to make sure the bear was really gone. I did the same again and again until I was only a few paces from the tent, which I circled before I entered it assured that the bear was not about.

It had been a trying experience, and for a long time I sat on a box, motionless, listening intently, slowly recovering my mental equilibrium.

Hours later Andrew returned with several boxes of explosives. And then George and Teddy arrived. I did not tell any of them about my encounter with the bear.

The weather deteriorated. It was now fifteen degrees above zero and fog, driven by a slow breeze, shrouded the surroundings in damp grayness.

I lay on my cot and was reading more of Dicken's Bleak House, as George got up — he had been sitting near the space heater — and said: "You could do other things than just read."

"What do you suggest?" I asked.

"Lay out a strip for the aircraft."

"Why?"

"That's a dumb question," he retorted. And as I grinned, he added: "That the pilot can land safely, that's why."

"In this kind of weather?" I kidded.

"It will clear shortly."

"I don't think so," I said, and went back to reading.

He muttered something — I caught the words 'lazy bugger' — donned his parka and left the tent. I heard him start a snowmobile and drive away. The din of the machine faded, became barely audible, then increased and faded time and again.

I put the book aside and went outside to have a look at what he was up to. The fog had settled down upon the surroundings. It was thicker than before, for I could not see anything beyond fifty feet. But that did not deter George from driving into the gray obscurity. He was attempting to level snowdrifts, to build an airstrip. I thought it an useless undertaking and a waste of gasoline. I returned to the tent.

There was no change in the weather during the following two days. I recorded a seismic shot; the rest of the time I read and tried to ignore George whose presence annoyed me. It was an unreasonable sentiment, but I could not help myself — I was on edge. The close quarter we had to share grated on my nerves.

Teddy had made pancakes for lunch and supper. Porridge was breakfast.

"Isn't there any meat?" George asked when we had pancakes for lunch again.

A can of coffee, a bag of tea, about one pound of brown sugar, some jam, pancake mix and oats were all the staples we had left. Teddy, Andrew and I were aware of it, but not George.

"There's bear meat if you want some," I replied with sarcasm.

"Don't be ridiculous," he scorned.

"But that's your only chance to eat meat," I said, then added: "Or you can drive to Table Island to fetch what I had to leave there and you didn't bring along."

"Explosives were more important than food," he defended himself.

"D'you think so?"

He shrugged his shoulder. "Then we do without

meat, won't we?"

I did not answer, neither did Teddy, and Andrew, I
was sure, had not understood. But I was wrong, for
moments later, smiling broadly and indicating with
the pointing finger of his right hand the squeezing
of a trigger, he said: "Kringmerk ... me boom ...
much nerkri."

What the devil! He's understood Geoge's remark, I
thought, and instantly realizing that there was the
chance of finding out whether George could speak
Eskimo, I asked: "What's kringmerk and nerkri?"

"You're having language lessons with him, not me.
So why don't you ask him," he replied with a grin.
Then he got up and strod out of the tent. And I
still did not know whether he spoke Andrew's tongue.
I tried to read the answer in Andrew's face, but he
only smiled. (Nerkri means food, meat).

A few hours later wind sprang up, blew for a while
in fitful gusts, then changed to a steady breeze. The
fog dissolved, and we could see the sky overcast and
the sun as a yellow speck near the horizon to the
southwest.

I stood outside the tent and watched Andrew feed
the dogs when the static crackle the loudspeaker
emitted broke off and, seconds later, Leon's voice
carried loud and clear in the air: "Are you guys
ready to record?"

Having figured that the improved weather would allow the Shooting Crew to prepare the shotpoints, the
call did not surprise me. I had checked out the recording spread and the instruments in advance. All
was functioning properly.

"This is Seismic 3. I'm ready to record," I transmitted, and heard Tony and Bill do the same.

Within the following few hours I recorded four
shots. The result was four, several feet long strips
of paper that showed what a layman would call: a mud-
dle of quivered lines. To me, however, they showed
that we continued mapping the thickness of the sedi-
ments on the bottom of the basin. I felt great satisfaction to participate in this scientific endeavor.

Before I switched the radio to standby, I asked
the aircraft dispatcher in Isachsen whether he would
send an aircraft my way, and if so, when that would
be?

"Sorry, Seismic 3. Cannot oblige. The weather's
down. But I'll send you one as soon as it improves,
— over."

With that, the retrieving by aircraft of the goods
I had left at Table Island had to be postponed. For
how long was uncertain. But we needed food, and that
within short time. I thought of doing it by dogsled
or snowmobile, but, recalling in my mind the ice condition we had met, I decided that it was too danger-

ous an undertaking. I raised the Shooting Crew instead and asked Leon to help me out with some meat
and canned vegetables.

"Sure. Send Teddy to get the stuff. And tell him
to bring along the powder which they dumped, — over,"
he transmitted.

Teddy left, and half an hour later, George. He
had stayed out of my hair, so to say, in everything I
had done and arranged. He told me he would be back
in a day or two. But why he was leaving and returning and where he was going to, he did not say, and I
did not ask.

After a while Andrew and I had language lesson.

It was past noon when Teddy returned.

"Me see two bears," he said as we unloaded the
boxes of grub he had received.

"How close were they?" I asked, uneasy about meeting bears again.

"Ten miles .. mebee more," he replied.

I sighed with relief.

"You not like bear?" he asked, and after the usual
pause, added: "Andrew shoot. Make good skin and much
meat for dogs."

"And that's exactly what I don't want!" I emphasized. "We'll be moving shortly and can't be bothered with hunting bears. You understand?"

Though he nodded, I knew that he could not under-

stand why I wanted to work when there was the prospect of a great hunt. I did not pursue the subject,
and after we had eaten a meal, this time: pork chops
and vegetables, we picked up the recording cable and
geophones.

We were loading the sleds as Andrew suddenly said:
"Taku!" and pointed westward. I remembered that taku
meant: look. I peered in the direction he was pointing. All I could see was a dark object on the horizon. It was too far away for me to make out what it
was. I hope it's not one of the bears Teddy's seen,
I thought, not pleased about such possibility.

"Atanerk," Andrew said.

"Atanerk?" I asked because I did not know what it
meant.

"George," he said, and I thought: that's baloney.
He's just kidding me.

I fetched my field glass and, really, it was
George. "Such eyesight ... that's incredible," I
muttered.

George was on foot and carried a jerrycan in his
left hand, but had no rifle with him.

"Teddy! Take the snowmobile and fetch him. And
hurry!" I urged.

"Thanks for picking me up," George said as he staggered off the snowmobile and flopped onto a sled. "I
ran out of gas," he added.

"How far from here?" I asked.

"Don't know," he groaned, looked at his watch, then added: "Must have walked three hours."

"Without the rifle? You sure take chances," I reproached, and as he made light of my saying so, I told him about the bears Teddy had sighted.

He paled. "I guess, you're right," he said, grinned and added: "This time."

"You're an ass," I retorted.

He grimaced. And that was all.

After another meal we struck camp. The load we distributed between the two sleds — one designed by the great explorer, Nansen, the other crafted by Eskimos.

(Nansen's design resembles a kamotik, though formed with modern materials and tools. It is an example, that careful consideration of the primitive and the modern can be very useful and prevent many failures).

Teddy was to pull the Nansen with the snowmobile. To the kamotik Andrew hitched his ten dogs. The question who would ride with whom was easily answered: George needed gasoline for his snowmobile, and the barrel containing it, was lashed onto Teddy's sled.

"I bet you two bits the snowmobile will be faster than the dogs," he said with a smile, and I accepted the wager.

I rode with Andrew. The ice was smooth and covered

with a thin layer of hard snow. It was ideal sledging and I enjoyed the ride for a time. After a few
miles, however, the surface became undulating and
then pack ice and pressure ridges loomed ahead. Teddy
and George had been faster and long since disappeared
from sight.

Andrew halted the dogs, stood up on the sled and
scanned with his eyes the ice ahead. I gathered that
he was looking for an easy route leading west. Then,
with nothing else than his guttural chant of orders,
he led the dogs in often long detours around the
roughest patches of up-heaved ice.

The sky was still overcast and the sun was still a
yellow speck that sent no perceptible warmth. A chilling breeze began to blow. I froze, and only when
the dogs floundered in snowdrifts and the sled got
stuck, compelling us to push, did I warm up.

The last miles before we reached our destination —
a tripod made of bamboo poles with orange ribbons
fluttering in the breeze, the marker for my next recording site — were smooth ice. The dogs did no more
flounder in drifts, the sled ran without getting
stuck, and there were no more warm-ups for me. I
suffered numbing cold because I was reluctant, perhaps
too proud, to call Andrew to stop, giving me a chance
to stomp my feet and thresh my arms.

He had much greater resistance to cold than I had.

I never saw him shiver, and I often felt admiration,
perhaps envy too, when he unraveled the dogs' traces
with bare hands, slapped them a few times as they became numb, then continued his task.

The Shooting Crew parked at the recording site.
Norman invited us to a meal.

"Before we pack up and head off," he said.

Andrew exchanged a few word with Edgar in their
tongue.

"He wants to look after his dogs first," the latter
explained, then turned to me: "Haven't you understood?"

"Nakka. But one day I might," I replied with a
grin.

"We heard that you two teach each other," Norman
said.

"Yes, we do."

"Trés bien, mon ami," Leon applauded. "Mais dites
moi, qu'est-ce dire, nakka?"

"On dit, non."

"Just listen to them jabber," Mike remarked, rather
testily.

I felt awkward and wanted to apologize for having
spoken in French he obviously did not understand. But
Leon beat me to it.

"Sorry, Mike. I got carried away," he said, chuckled, then went on: "We didn't talk about you, if

that's what's bothering you. I simply asked what
nakka means."

"Yeah? Then what does it mean?" Mike demanded.

"No," Leon said.

"What no?" Mike snapped, angrily.

"Au diable! Are you deaf? I said ... it means,
no! Do you get it now?" Leon exploded.

The argument had suddenly become heated. There's
really no reason for that. Leon and I often exchange
a few words in his tongue, I thought, drowsily. Overcome by unaccustomed warmth, and being tired, I was
on the verge of dozing off.

But Norman's: "Hey, you two! Quit it!" roused me.
I yawned and stretched myself.

He smiled. "It happens to all of us sometimes,"
he said.

He postponed the departure of his crew because he
wanted to wait for George and Teddy to arrive.

"One can never be sure that all goes as planned,"
he told me. He was a decent fellow.

In the meantime, Andrew pitched his tent, moved
his stuff into it, then helped me to pitch mine. Not
leaving it to chance, and ignoring George's objection, I had loaded it with my cot and sleeping bag
and some grub onto the kamotik. And now I was glad I
had done it.

Edgar came and watched us. I got the impression

that he wanted to tell me something, but did not know
how to begin.

"I'm listening," I encouraged.

"I'd like you to understand," he started, paused,
then went on: "Normally, we're gettin' along quite
well. But lately we've been workin' hard and everybody's tired and that's when tempers are likely to
flare up."

"I understand," I replied and smiled.

"I'm glad you do. Was thinkin' that you might
have gotten the wrong impression ... that we're a
fightin' bunch of guys," he said and turned away.
But after a few steps he came back.

"I heard that you and George also have it out from
time to time. I'd like to listen in, sometimes."

I laughed. "I bet you would."

Several hours passed before George and Teddy arrived with only one snowmobile and the sled. They
were visibly tired.

All of us assembled in the kitchen and listened to
George telling us about their struggles. Shortly
after entering the ice pack, they found the Shooting
Crew's tracks wiped out by blown snow. Having thus
lost the advantage of following an existing route,
they had to find their own way now. The snowmobiles
got stuck in deep, loose snow or spun out on glare
ice. When crossing pressure ridges, the sled often

ran free and spilled its load. Gathering up the wide-
ly scattered items and loading them onto the sled
again, sapped their strength. And to make it worse,
Teddy's snowmobile quit running, and the advantage of
pulling the sled in tandem was lost.

"And all that time the breeze got colder and colder. We almost froze to death," he concluded.

I was sorting out cables and geophones — Teddy was
sleeping in our tent — as George approached.

"You beat us. Here's the quarter," he said, smiling tiredly, and handed me the piece. "What's your
plan?" he then asked, hesitantly.

"Lay out the spread. Why d'you ask?"

"Then you don't mind if I sleep on your cot?"

"No. Go ahead."

"I'm really tuckered out," he said and staggered
toward the tent.

Norman had been waiting within earshot. He approached now.

"There's some meat and other stuff," he said and
put down a box. "It's all we can spare. But it
should last you a few days, at least till you'll get
more from Isachsen."

He gave a nod in George's direction. "I heard him.
He's sure tame. Wonder how long it lasts."

"Who knows?" I returned. "And thanks for the grub."

"Be seeing you," he said and left, but after a few

steps he halted and turned around. "I've left you a battery generator and half a drum of gasoline," he called and pointed to where he had left them on the ice.

Then he walked to his vehicle, climbed into the seat and gave the signal to move on. The engines ran up, gears ground shortly, the tracks began to roll with clattering noise — the entire outfit headed west.

The noise faded, the vehicles and sleds vanished from sight. There was silence and a limitless, white horizon again.

For a long time I stood and gazed wonderingly into the seeming endlessness. And while I gazed, the long repressed desire to experience that endlessness, to travel beyond the white horizon, rose in me again. I realized that though long views always charmed me, no wild horizon ever fascinated me as much as the white one did. And all the subtle emotions that had yielded to hard facts returned and conjured up fancies drawn from my recent experiences. I shuddered, and reality returned.

Once again I had no help laying out the recording spread and putting up the radio masts. George and Teddy were sleeping, and Andrew left with his dogs in pursuit of a bear we saw ambling across the ice.

"No kill nanuk!" I protested.

But he just smiled, and all my gesticulations in

lieu of appropriate words in his tongue did not help
to change his mind. I reckoned that his ancestral
instinct compelled him to go after the bear and nothing else mattered.

In addition to reels and geophones I carried now
also my rifle. Although the bear disappeared over
the horizon to the east of us, I did not think it
wise to be unarmed.

Hours later, having laid out the spread, set up
the radio masts and strung the antenna between them,
I was worn-out. Not thinking of the two sleepers, I
started the generator to charge the batteries, then
entered the tent to hook them up.

"You woke me! Couldn't that have waited?" George
complained.

I looked at my watch.

"You've slept five hours! That's long enough!" I
barked, angrily, and turned to make coffee.

"Are you touchy. I didn't mean to upset you," he
muttered.

Blob ... blob ... blob, burst the bubbles in the
glass knob of the coffee pot's lid. This sound, combined with the aroma of percolating coffee, restored
my composure.

"D'you want some?" I asked.

Still lying in his bag, arms out of it, hands
folded in the nape of his neck, he stared at the

ceiling of the tent.

"Yes, I do," he said, and then asked: "How's the
weather?"

"Overcast. And a nasty wind's blowing," I replied, and handed him a mugful of coffee.

After a few sips he called: "Hey, Teddy! Wake up!
We've work to do!"

Teddy had not stirred in spite of all the loud
noises.

"What work? I've done it all," I blurted out.

"Oh. Then you got his snowmobile?" he taunted,
and before I could answer, he said: "Never mind,
we'll go and get it."

"But you'll eat first, won't you?" I joked.

After they had left I stopped the generator, turned the space heater's knob to low, switched the radio
to standby, and without undressing myself took a
rest. I slept until the din of a snowmobile woke me
about three hours later.

I rushed outside. George had returned.

"Where's the toolbox?" he demanded without preliminaries, checked himself, then added: "We were halfway when I remembered having left it here."

"And you left Teddy out there without sleeping bag
or any kind of shelter?" I exclaimed.

"There's no risk in that. I'll be back there in
no time at all," he countered.

I was astounded about the lack of concern he displayed, but kept my mouth shut because I knew that
any objection would lead to a heated argument that
would solve nothing, only create ill-feelings we did
not need. He seemed to sense my thoughts , for he
said, somewhat amicably: "I couldn't raise you on the
radio. You keep it on standby, don't you?"

I did not mention I had slept, but wondered why I
had not heard his transmission. Habitually a light
sleeper, I was always instantly roused by voice or
noise.

"The signal's been weak. I guess the radio's on
the blink," I said.

"Can't you fix it?"

"I haven't tried yet."

"Then leave it to me. I'll take care of it," he
said, and put the toolbox into the snowmobile.

I ran into the tent to get his and Teddy's sleeping bag, but he had driven off when I returned.

"Oh, why do I bother?" I muttered, feeling dis-
gusted. Perhaps I'm too cautious, I went on to myself. But Andrew took along his bag. So? Am I
wrong or is George taking too many risks that might
prove detrimental one day?

Some time later I stood outside the tent again and
gazed about the monotonous, white expanse and wondered where Andrew and the other fellows were. The

wind moaned and the snow drifted. And suddenly — I
did not know why — I thought of friends and acquaintances who told me how they envied me for doing what
they would also do if they had the chance.

A chance they wanted!

But would they take it or just stay home and read
with gratitude, perhaps admiration, stories about the
wanderers of the world — the explorers, sailors and
vagabonds — knowing little of their real lot: the
restlessness that compels them to move on, to see, to
discover; the weariness that follows, but does not
keep them to rest long.

In my heart of hearts I knew that I was one of
these wanderers. And I asked myself whether my
friends and acquaintances who were so envious of my
doing were wanderers, too? I doubted it and shoved
these thoughts into the back of my mind.

I returned to the tent to attend to my frostbitten face. The lips were chapped and blistered. Nose
and cheeks were dark-blotched with peeling skin that
showed new, pink tissue. The ears, likewise blotched
with peeling skin, their lobes were swollen, a yellow
secretion forming a crust on them.

Many times before had my face been frostbitten,
and so I knew that nothing less than medicated cream
would relieve the painful throbbing, prevent the
cracking of new tissue and speed up healing.

I had a tube of such cream, but it was frozen.
Nevertheless, I tried to spread lumps of it over the
sores. But the least pressure from my trembling finger hurt more than doing good. I gave up and thought
of softening the cream. I heated water and when it
boiled dropped the tube into it. Before I realized
that this was a mistake, the tube burst and cream
coated the water filling the inside of the tent with
the smell of infirmary. Furious, I grabbed the pot
and flung it out of the tent where its content spilled onto the ice.

Having lost the cream, I reverted to what could be
called the old-fashioned treatment of sores. I dissolved powdered milk in lukewarm water and dabbed the
sores with the mixture from time to time. It relieved the pain and the sores began to heal.

Near the camp was the remnant of an old pressure
ridge. It was covered with snowdrifts, and only the
odd big chunk of up-heaved ice reminded of its presence. These chunks were vantage points.

As the hours passed and I became increasingly uneasy about the whereabout of George and Teddy who
were out there without any means of shelter, I made
frequent trips to one, climbed it and scanned with
the binoculars the ice until my hands became numb and
the eyes began to water, blurring my sight.

It was late afternoon as I spotted Andrew and his

team of dogs. They were traveling straight for the camp. There was, however, still no sign of George and Teddy, and I resolved, should they not have returned by midnight, to send Andrew looking for them.

I was lying on my cot and was reading a copy of Steinbeck's Sweet Thursday when, an hour or so later, Andrew's arrival was heralded by the dogs' short yelps, their panting and the squeal of the sled. I put aside the paperback and left the tent to have a look at his bounty. But no bear skin and no meat was lashed onto the sled.

"No nanuk?" I asked.

He looked straight at me and there was no smile on his lips. "Nakka," he said in a low tone, bent down and began switching the dogs from their traces to their respective chain tethers.

I was glad the bear had escaped, but did not show or voice my emotion because he seemed downcast for having failed to bag the bear. Later, when we had eaten and then had language lesson, he said: "Many nanuk," and pointed to the outside. I understood that he meant to say that there were many bears about and he would get one or more, sooner or later. He had overcome his disappointment.

I was sketching items that were parts of our daily life on the ice and whose names in Eskimo I wanted to know, as he turned his head away and listened intently.

"Atanerk ... come," he said, got up and left the tent.

Remembering that atanerk meant boss, I followed him. There was nobody in sight nor could I hear the din of snowmobiles.

"Andrew, you're ... you're ...." I faltered and then stopped speaking, for I raked my memory for the word he had told me and would mean: is wrong. It was a word that had taken me quite some time to understand because I could not sketch adjectives, verbs or adverbs and could only learn through gesticulations.

"Tammarpok!" I burst out, pleased that the word had come to me.

He shook his head and, smiling broadly, pointed at my ear.

"No good ... siudluktok," he said.

It was another word he had told me, and which meant: hears with difficulty or: is of hard hearing.

I cupped the ears with my hands and, there! — I heard a sound that rose and fell by turns and I recognized as the din of snowmobiles. Not only has he keener eyesight, but also better hearing than myself, I thought, slightly envious.

Minutes later the snowmobiles came in sight. I could not make out who was leading because vehicles

and drivers looked the same, except the trailing unit
was pulling a sled. Teddy's following George, I
thought.

And right I was — George arrived first. He got
off the snowmobile and without as much as giving a
sign that he had seen us, rushed into the tent.

Wondering what he was up to, I followed him. He
stared at the radio.

"It **is** on standby!" he hissed through clenched
teeth, turned to me, and rapped: "What's wrong with
that blasted thing? Or were you too lazy to answer?"
His voice trembled with repressed anger.

"Dammit! I told you it spooks," I retorted and,
all of a sudden, I found the situation rather ridiculous and began to laugh.

"What's so funny?" he snapped.

"Nothing. I'm just feeling good that you and
Teddy are back," I evaded, determined to prevent a
row.

He glared at me, then turned away and left the
tent.

"Now don't go far if you want to eat! I'm cooking!" I called after him.

Teddy had come in and was changing his footwear.

"What bit him? And why are you guys so late?" I
asked.

He glanced at the entrance. "Him crazy," he said,

curtly, and resumed changing his footwear.

I knew better than to pursue the matter. In time
he would tell me what had happened. But I never
found out because I went seal hunting with Andrew,
and when I returned, the incident had escaped my
mind, and Teddy did not bring it up.

"I'll repair the radio tomorrow," George said
while he and Teddy were eating the meal I had prepared. "I want to have some shut-eye first," he ·
added.

"Then I go seal hunting with Andrew. We need food
for the dogs," I said, and after a pause, asked:
"Will you record the shot if there's one?"

He stared at me, and I grew afraid he would refuse.
But, surprising me, he said with pronounced deliber-
ateness: "I don't mind ... this time."

"Now that's being a real pal," I kidded.

He gaped and I grinned. "So long," I said and
left the tent.

"Don't stay away too long!" he called after me.

I helped Andrew load the sled. We had agreed by
means of our scant knowledge of each other's tongue
and supported by gestures, that we would go hunting
seal. It was something I was looking forward to experience.

We sledged north. The weather was spring-lie warm,
almost muggy. The snow on top of the ice was soft

and wet. The runners of the sled sank deep, taxing
the dogs' strength and endurance. Andrew encouraged
them with: "Attai! Attai!" or when he saw a slack
trace he flicked the whip and hit the offender with
deadly accuracy. I observed that they hopped less
frequently over each other's traces or ducked underneath them than during the previous travels when the
snow had been dry. The forming of a plait was thus
less frequent. But when it happened, Andrew unraveled it with his usual patience.

Our camp had long since disappeared from sight,
and I began to wonder whether the area we were heading for was frequented by seal. I was on the verge
of voicing my doubts as Andrew pointed and ordered
the dogs to stop. To my naked eye there was just a
dark spot visible, and only through the binoculars
could I make out that it was a seal resting next to
its breathing hole. Such keen eyesight. I wish I
had it, too, I thought and kept on glassing the seal.

Standing on the sled, he watched the seal for a
long time. Then he jumped down and out of his blue
box, lashed to the front of the sled, he took a rolled-up, white cloth which he spread on the snow. It
was roughly four-foot square and had triangular pockets at each corner. After his unsuccessful bear hunt
I had seen him cut pieces from discarded bamboo
poles, but had not asked what he would use them for.

He pulled now three of them from under the tarpaulin and inserted two into these pockets diagonally across the sheet to hold it taut. The third piece, which he had capped on one end with a piece of cloth, he pushed into the center of the sheet, bulging it out. With a piece of string he fastened it at the intersection of the other two. The assembly formed a shield with a long handle at its center.

He checked his rifle, a Lee Enfield 303, took up the shield, smiled and motioned for me to stay with the dogs. To approach the seal upwind, he walked in a wide circle around it.

Watching the seal through the binoculars, I saw that it was what could be called a fitful sleeper. It lay still, apparently asleep, then suddenly rose its head, looked all around and if it found that all was safe slumped down to sleep again. After a minute or so, it awoke to do the same, time and again.

With growing excitement I watched Andrew stalk it. Each time it lifted its head he ducked behind the shield. The instance it slumped down to sleep he walked quickly toward it. In this manner he slowly closed in on it. At a distance of about one hundred feet he waited during several sequences of the seal's routine, and as it had, once again, slumped down, I saw his rifle come up over the shield and shortly after I heard a faint crack. The seal's plump body

heaved spasmodically and then lay still. He had killed it with one shot.

(Weeks later, when I had an opportunity to talk
with Edgar and told him about the hunt, he told me
that it is imperative to kill the seal with one shot
or it will, even if fatally wounded , make it to the
breathing hole and slip down it not to be found by
the hunter).

While Andrew had stalked the seal, the dogs had
watched him, leering intently, whimpering, their
bodies raked by spasmodic shivers. At the moment
they heard the shot they sprang up and raced off so
fast that I toppled from the sled and landed on the
ice. Cursing them with a litany of abusive exclama-
tions, I ran after them, but gave up shortly because
they were racing too fast for me to catch up.

When I reached Andrew he had disassembled the
shield, had stored it on the sled, and had slit open
the seal. It was a big ringed seal — I recognized it
as such, for it had white spots with dark centers.

He squatted beside it, cut pieces off the steam-
ing liver and ate them with snippets of blubber. He
offered me a small piece of the bloody, slippery
liver. I felt revulsion grip me. But not wanting to
show my queasiness, I took and swallowed it. I sup-
pose it was more the thought of eating it raw that
made me gag than its taste which was not bad at all.

Since I did not throw up and was hungry, I ate more of it and also bits of blubber, the taste of which was bland and slightly sweet.

For almost two months I had lived exclusively on frozen meat, cereals and canned goods, and found now a certain dietary satisfaction in eating raw blubber and raw liver.

Our faces and hands smeared with blood, we had more the looks of two primeval hunters squatting over their bloody bounty and gorging raw meat, than members of a civilized world. And all of a sudden it seemed to me that the savage in me, some leftover from a distant past when the hunt had been a necessity for survival, had cropped up again and derived satisfaction from this crude act. I thought of friends and fellow workers of former years and wondered how they would react seeing me the way they would never be. Mirth rose in me and I began to laugh, and Andrew, not knowing why I laughed, smiled.

After we had eaten our fill he gutted the carcass and distributed the intestines among the dogs who had watched us with saliva dripping from their jaws. They gulped down the pieces so fast that none had a chance to fight the other for its possession.

Not knowing Andrew's plan, I pointed whence we had come and asked: "Tamamnuk ... tupperk?", words that meant: both of us ... tent? He smiled, and that was

all. He had not grasped the meaning of what I wanted
to say: are we going back to camp? I repeated the
words, but with corresponding gestures this time.
His eyes, normally mere slits, opened wide for an instance and his smile grew wider.

He got it! He got it! I triumphed silently.

He shook his head. "No. Much netserk ... seal,"
he said , and with a sweep of his right encircled the
area to the north and east.

I understood we would hunt more seal. That meant
to travel again until he, perhaps I myself, would
spot some of them. I checked my watch — it was more
than six hours since we had left camp. George won't
be happy about me staying away longer, I thought and
felt guilty for a moment.

Andrew walked to the carcass and motioned for me
to help him load it onto the sled. Having done it,
he squatted beside the sled and smoked a cigarette,
and I lay stretched out on the ice and watched the
clouds change their shapes while they slowly drifted
past.

Then we traveled north, and after a few miles I
saw the dark outlines of the southern coast of Ellef
Ringness Island. Andrew halted the dogs, stood up on
his blue box — it was the highest point on the sled —
and glassed the distant area.

"No netserk," he said at length and jumped down.

The dogs got up, he broke out the sled, hopped on
it, and at his command they hurled themselves into
the traces. We were on the way again.

"Hoie! Hoie!" he encouraged. The dogs swung to
the right, eastward, toward Hendriksen Strait.

"Andrew! Netserk there?" I called.

He wagged his head, and I gathered that he did not
know if there were seal.

The hours wore on. I stared at the monotonous un-
dulations of wind-blown snow until drowsiness over-
came me and my eyelids began to droop. The surroundings blurred, darkened, the squeal of the runners
switched to faraway musical tunes — I fell asleep.

How much later it was as I aroused at Andrew's
call: "Nanuk!", I did not know. He pointed at a
spoor, and there was a slight tremor of excitement in
his voice as he repeated: "Nanuk!"

The paw prints were inches larger than my mukluks.

"And a big nanuk!" I burst out.

"Ima," he said and smiled, then changed the course
to follow the bear's spoor.

"Attai! Attai!" he spurred on the dogs while he
stood on the pitching sled, balancing with bent knees
and scanning with his eyes the ice, which was getting
rougher with every passing mile.

Ahead was pressure ice, an area of crushed and
tumbled ice blocks, some twenty perhaps more feet

high, the spaces between them full of smaller pieces
sticking out of deep snow. It was the result of early winterstorms that had raged across the Arctic when
the cold had not numbed the sea yet.

The spoor headed for that nightmarish jumble, and
I did not like the idea of entering it because I
thought it far too risky to do so. To my relief the
spoor veered south where, as far as I could make out,
the ice was smooth and no obstructions loomed on the
horizon.

The weather changed. The clouds darkened and wind
sprang up. The sun hung above the horizon as a small,
cold and cheerless yellow spot. There was no more
softness in the air — harsh and unrelenting was the
climate's disposition again.

All of a sudden the dogs began to yelp and whine
and to pull with renewed eagerness. They winded the
bear. I peered ahead, and there he was, not more
than half a mile distant. He padded in a shuffling
gait across the ice.

Andrew sidled to the front of the sled and released
the dogs, pulled his rifle from under the tarpaulin
and ran behind them.

Excitement gripped me — I joined the hunt.

Resembling furry balls, the dogs streaked toward
the bear. Andrew let go a bloodcurdling scream, and
I ran panting , stumbling and slipping, my lungs on

155

the brink of bursting.

Alarmed by the ongoing commotion, the bear stopped
his amble, peered during a few moments, then turned
and fled in a rolling, ungainly gallop. But it was
too late for him — he did not escape the snarling,
snapping canines. They danced around him, darted in
and out, harassing their lumbering, charging foe.
They held him at bay. He swatted at the crazed dogs
or made short charges with his jaws agape. It was a
battle scene that was ferocious and undisguised by
human emotion — it fascinated and at once repulsed me.

Andrew ran close to the bear, took aim and shot,
worked the action of his rifle and fired again. The
bear rolled on his side, tried to rise with a snarl,
but collapsed. A convulsive shudder ran through his
massive body, and then he lay lifeless.

As I caught up all was quiet. The dogs, short moments earlier raging furies, lay in a half circle
around their foe. They knew that the bear was dead,
yet they glowered, ready to attack should he revive.

Appraising his bounty, Andrew prodded the bear
with his foot. "Much big," he said, obviously proud.

Looking at this magnificent carnivore — a king
among its kind — regret assailed me and I wished the
hunt would not have happened.

After retrieving the sled, I made tea, and we ate
pieces of blubber from the seal. (During the following

months I ate raw blubber whenever Andrew killed seal
for the dogs. I knew that it was rich in Vitamin C.
And every time I ate of it I thought of Nelly and her
concern about me getting scurvy).

Andrew skinned the bear, slowly and carefully. It
took hours to do it, and when the skin was spread out
on the ice I estimated it to be in excess of twelve
feet from head to tail.

Though dead, there still had been the strength and
magnificence in the bear. But now, looking at the
pink, flayed body, I shuddered in disgust and wondered
whither the strength and magnificence had gone.

When Andrew had gutted and cut up the carcass he
fed some of its meat and guts to the dogs. The rest
of the entrails and the liver he left on the ice far
from the dogs' reach. (The polar bear liver is often
so rich in Vitamin A that it is poisonous. Human who
eat it can die of hypervitaminosis. Dogs get sick
and lose their hair if they are fed with it or will
get it by other means).

We had now enough seal and bear meat to feed the
dogs for many days. There was no more need to hunt
another seal. Therefore, we turned back to camp.

The wind had picked up in strength, making it very
cold — the wet, soft snow crusted over. The crust
supported the dogs, but the sled broke frequently
through it. Andrew and I walked beside it and

157

assisted the dogs whenever this happened. After several miles and no prospect of getting onto snow that would support the sled, we unloaded almost three quarter of the bear meat. Through gesticulations I understood that he would return to recover it.

George did not fuss about my prolonged absence. His only remark was: "You're very late."

When I told him about the hunt he eyed me with obvious disgust and said that I had the looks of primitive man: a terrible face with peeling skin and blood-crusted blotches, unkempt hair and beard, and wore a greasy, blood-splattered cloth, meaning my parka, and was a real disgrace to any civilized being. Though he could have been a bit more tactful about it, I accepted his bluntness with equanimity because he was right.

He had not found the problem that affected the radio's flawless functioning, had however, plowed an airstrip, what meant: he had leveled snowdrifts with driving the snowmobile across them.

"Three aircraft are on the way. They'll bring explosives," he said.

"What about the food and fuel I ordered?" I asked.

"First we get the explosives, and then you get your stuff," was his answer.

"Why must we get the powder and not the Shooting Crew?" I objected.

"Because they're in pack ice and so we bring it to
them."

"Who's we?"

"I and Teddy and Andrew," he replied, then added
with a grin: "I guess you won't mind being alone for
a few days."

"What can I say? You decided, and that's that,
right?"

Before he could answer the loudspeaker emitted a
garbled message. I took the microphone from its hook,
but George snatched it from my hand. I shrugged my
shoulder and left the tent. Before I had moved out
of earshot I heard him repeat his transmission several times.

I watched the sky to the west and listened intently. And then I heard a faint hum and saw a dot low
over the horizon. The hum increased, so did the dot,
and moments later the aircraft thundered over the
camp, banked sharply, leveled its wings and touched
down to bounce and sway, the wing tips almost hitting
the surface of the ice where George had marked the
airstrip with poles. My heart leapt in terror and
with my mind's eye I saw the aircraft in bits and
pieces strewn over the ice. I heard the engine run
up, saw the aircraft bounce a few more times, then
settle on its tail wheel while still gliding forward
in a slight zigzag course. After it had slowed down

it turned around and taxied to where I stood.

The engine run up once more, quit, the propeller rumbling to its stop. The cockpit door flung open, the pilot jumped down. His face ablaze with rage, he yelled: "What no-good-for-nothing, stupid ...,"

"Don't yell at me!" I interrupted.

He startled. "I should have known," he then said, pulled off the gloves and proffered his right.

"We haven't met. I'm Chuck," he introduced himself.

He was a lanky fellow of my height, possibly the same age, had an energetic face, blue eyes and dark-blond hair. He wore a white flight overall and fur-lined boots.

"Where is he?" he demanded.

"What's he done?"

"Dammit! Didn't you see it? I almost wrecked the plane because he told me that he'd prepared a strip that was without bumps. That ...." He checked himself, then asked: "Where's your radio? I must warn Stu and Dale. They'll be coming soon."

I gave a nod toward the tent. Without saying another word, he left and shortly after I heard angry voices.

Teddy and Andrew helping me, we unloaded the aircraft in short order. The freight was food, fuel and explosives. Then we joined George and Chuck who had settled their differences and were having tea.

"The plane's unloaded," I said.

"Thanks," Chuck replied, and I got the impression that he was surprised, but also pleased that we had done it without his help.

"Seismic 3. What's your altimeter and wind?" pealed the radio.

George shot up, tapped the altimeter, took a brief look at the outside, then transmitted his observation.

"That was Stu. I better be going," Chuck said, emptied his cup and got up.

I walked with him to the aircraft. Before we reached it he stopped abruptly. "Sorry, I almost forgot," he said, reached in his pocket and handed me two letters. I recognized the handwriting on them — it was Nelly's. I felt as if I had received the best gift I could have wished for.

Hours later everybody had left. I was alone. Clouds rose in the west and slowly spread across the sky, hiding its blue and enveloping the country in gloom. The temperature, well below freezing, climbed rapidly. Then squall after squall of snow mixed with rain scudded across the ice. They ended as abruptly as they had begun, and thick fog moved in. It was the twenty-first of May and this fast changing, moody weather was the first sign of the impending breakup.

I worked on seismic records when, suddenly, the

eerie silence was rent by a querulous wail outside the tent. I froze, but listened intently. There! I heard it again. A mixture of fear and curiosity gripped me. I tiptoed to the entrance, peered through the flaps, gasped in disbelief and rushed out, yelling: "Get the hell away from my stuff!" and without giving it a second thought, gave the bear, who stood near the pile of supplies and was sniffing its scent, a boot in the rear. It was a female bear, for two cubs backed away, frightened. She gave a grunt, pawed at her cubs, and scuttled off with the small ones scurrying between her legs.

I watched them go, and not before the fog had swallowed them did I realize what I had done. My heart palpitated, goose bumps ran up and down my arms, my knees weakened — I shuffled to the pile of supplies and flopped onto a box. There I sat motionless while my mind hammered: boot a polar bear in the ass? Crazy! Stupid! Lunatic! Ready for the nuthouse!

Fortunately, the bears had approached the camp downwind or they might otherwise have smelled the meat Andrew had left in a pile or my cache of pork chops and sausages, and I would not have gotten away with simply booting mama bear. This rash action could have spelled my end. I had been very, very lucky.

CHAPTER 6

It was early morning when I left the tent for a
recess in the old pressure ridge — our temporary
privy. The fog had lifted, revealing a day that was
gray and chill. The snow, slushy a few hours earlier,
was frozen, giving my steps a crunching sound. Beyond the ridge stretched snow-covered rough first year
ice. Loath to return to camp directly, I took a
roundabout stroll over part of it.

Crossing a snowdrift, I came upon large and small
paw prints. Yesterday's mother bear with her cubs,
shot through my head. I turned and fled over the ice,
stumbling and slipping, expecting to hear a growl and
to feel the swat that would plunge me into oblivion —
end my life.

But I want to live! my inner voice cried. You
know bears ... don't run ... face her ... shout ...
wave you arms ... jump up and down ... rave ... she
might scare. Take heart and do it ... just don't run!
the voice insisted.

But ..., my mind protested.

No buts ... do it! Coward! the voice burst out,
silently.

Coward? That stung my ego.

"I'm no coward!" I cried, stopped running and turned around to face a scenery empty of bear.

I sighed with relief, for, once again, I had left
the rifle in the tent.

The tracks were fresh, or so it seemed. Where are
the bears? Have they smelled the meat cache, the
pile Andrew left, and are raiding them now? What can
I do without rifle? All these questions raced through
my mind while, unsure of what to expect, I shuffled
stealthily toward the old pressure ridge that blocked
my view of the camp.

"Oh, good," I breathed.

The bears were not there, nor was there any sign
that they had visited.

I ran down the slope, rushed into the tent, grabbed
the rifle and hurried up to the hummock I used as
lookout. From there I watched the ice till I was convinced that no bear was near, and pangs of hunger reminded me that I had not had breakfast yet.

I worked again on the seismic records, but found
it impossible to concentrate on them. Time after time
my thoughts turned to the bears I had met at close
quarter, and dwelled upon the possibility of different
outcomes.

Though I reasoned with myself that another encounter with one of them was unlikely, I made frequent
trips to the lookout to make sure that no bear was in
the vicinity.

Toward evening I received the radio message that

George, Teddy and Andrew had reached the Shooting Crew, and without having lost a pound of explosives.

"Stand by, you guys. We'll be ready with the shot in no time," Leon added to the message.

But, "in no time", turned out to be several hours.

"Sorry about that. We broke a drill stem. That's why it took that long," he replied when Tony kidded him about having used the wrong phrase.

Thereafter, I had no time to think of bears, for during the following sixteen hours I was busy with recording, developing the records, drying and checking them.

I had eaten and was ready to turn in when Teddy returned alone.

"Much driving," he said and slumped onto his cot.

Then he told me that George would not join us again before we had moved to the next recording site, and that Andrew was trailing behind.

"Me faster. No see him when here," he said, and I detected pride in his voice.

I asked him if he wanted to eat right away, in which case I would cook a meal for him.

"No. Wait for Andrew. Make coffee now," he replied.

Then he left to fetch ice, our store of water. And while he was gone, I turned in.

The yelping of dogs woke me. It seemed to me as if I had just closed my eyes, yet I had slept four

165

hours. Teddy, fully clothed, was sleeping on his cot.
The arrival of Andrew with the dogs and the ensuing
clamor did not arouse him.

Sometime later the three of us sat down to the meal
I had prepared.

"Much netserk ... seal. Me go shoot," Andrew said
when we had downed the last morsel.

Using the same lingo, I said: "Soon ... weather ...
much bad. Better stay here."

He smiled and I wondered whether he had understood.
But after a prolonged pause, he said: "No ... go ...
dog eat." It meant he needed dog food.

I assumed that he had seen seal, but for unexplain-
ed reason had not bagged one or two. And now, having
fed the last of the bear meat to the dogs, he was going to hunt, bad weather or not. Although he seemed
to be tired from the long drive, he did not rest, but
made preparations for an immediate departure.

Teddy helped him, then came to me and said: "Me go
with Andrew. Okay?"

There was no work for him until I had recorded the
last shot for my present location, and waiting for it
could take days.

"Okay. But take our small tent along," I said, re-
signed to the fact that I would be alone again.

He hesitated, then asked why they should take along
the tent; that they were not going to camp, only to

hunt for seal. I told him that I was sure a storm
was coming and they ought to have a shelter in case
they were caught in it.

"Okay ... boss," he said, flatly.

Damn you, I thought, annoyed at his apparent in-
difference, which sometimes disconcerted me.

The dogs, fed and rested, yelped and squirmed in
eager anticipation as Andrew tied them to their
traces, and at his command hurled themselves forward,
galloping at first, then settling down to a steady
trot. I watched from the lookout until men and dogs
had disappeared over the northwesterly horizon. Then,
convinced that a storm was coming, I secured the camp.

Hours earlier, the sky had been blue with a bright,
cheerful sun. Now it was clouded over and looked
leaden, threatening. There was no wind. An oppres-
sive calm lay over the white expanse. The barometer
was slowly dropping; the mercury stood at fourteen
degrees.

The blizzard was not long in coming. It started
with a sudden gust of wind that whirled up snow. It
passed and for a while calm prevailed again. A second
gust blew up. Resembling veiled, fleet dancers, snow
whirled past. There came a third, a forth, a fifth
burst of wind, each stronger and lasting longer than
the one before. And then a steadily increasing blast
obscured the surroundings in blowing, drifting snow.

The hours wore on. Fully dressed, I lay on my cot,
watched the canvas of the tent bulge and slack, listened to the raging, howling wind, thought of a multi-
tude of things unrelated to the presence and, finally,
fell asleep.

An icy blast woke me with a start. How long I had
slept I did not care to check, for the tent flapped
wildly and wind shrieked about me. Instantly, I realized what had happened — the storm had bared the
ground flap on the weather side and torn it from the
pegs, and only the guy ropes held the tent from top-
pling over.

The space heater sizzled. I rushed from the cot
and turned it off. Rather cold than have I fire, I
thought distraught.

The icy, violent wind thwarted my attempt to weigh
down the flap and to cover it with snow on the outside. I could not do it alone!

Though I was freezing, I forced myself to calm,
deliberate action, the only way to save myself from
disaster.

I thought of abandoning the tent and to move into
Andrew's, yet discarded that notion as fast as it had
risen because I knew that the racing, blinding squalls
of snow would instantly engulf me and I would lose
orientation, neither find his tent nor be able to re-
trace my steps. I would not have a chance and would

simply freeze to death.

As every storm is bent on destruction, so was this one. I feared a gust would lift the tent with its frame off the ice and blow it into a heap of bent pipes and flapping canvas. I had to weigh it down!

But how am I to do that? I cried, silently, desperate to think of a solution.

Teddy's sled! shot through my head.

Tied with ropes to the upper pipes of the frame and raised a foot or more off the ice, it would serve as a suspended platform, and loaded with the instruments, a few crates and boxes filled with supplies, it would hold the tent from lifting off. I could spread my sleeping bag on top — and all would be safe!

By the time I had done all these things and lay shivering in my bag, my fingers were frozen stiff, resembled grappling hooks, and my face was frostbitten again. There had been moments when I had lain on the ice, spent and on the verge of giving up. But the will to live, to overcome the tremendous physical punishment the storm inflicted on me, had made me crawl, heave and push.

After a while I stopped shivering, the fingers unbent and, like my face, began to glow. I lay in the bag, watched, wondered and dozed by turns.

There was no letup in the storm's violence. It howled and raged. It sounded as if the gates of

Dante's hell had opened and I could hear the shriek-
ing and lamenting souls damned to suffer in eternity.
The tent shook and groaned, and its canvas flapped
wildly under the relentless onslaught of the gusts.
But it stood fast, held by the guy ropes and the
weight of the suspended sled-platform.

During two days and a half raged the blizzard.
Then it belonged to the past — the elements were
serene again. The clouds parted and revealed blue
sky with the sun bright, cheerful.

The inside of the tent looked like a snow-cave in
which my sleeping bag and everything else was covered
with a thick layer of snow. A deep drift reached
from the space heater beyond the entrance.

I dug and cleared, brushed clean and set up; connected cables, troubled over the lightning of the
space heater and the starting of the battery charger;
walked along the mile of recording cable, checked
geophones for proper hookup; tested instruments and
line, and when all was functioning properly, and the
tent was warm again, I cooked a meal and ate it. Then
I transmitted my readiness to record the next seismic
shot.

"Had much damage? Seismic 3," Tony asked.

"The usual things, — over," I hedged.

"So you were not blown away?" Bill sent, then added: "For your information: it piped up to sixty-five."

(This meant: miles per hour).

"I recorded not over sixty," Tony informed.

"This is the Shooting Crew. It was really bad ... well over sixty," Edgar intercepted.

"Two to one. Check your instrument, Seismic 1. I bet it's busted," Bill kidded.

There was a pause, then Tony's voice came loud and clear: "It's possible. But more important ... Shooting Crew, when will you be ready to fire the shot? I'd like to move to Cape Isachsen before breakup, — over."

"We're loading now. Perhaps in an hour, — over," Edgar informed.

"Standing by," Tony transmitted, and so did Bill and I.

An hour later we recorded the shot.

"How's that for time? — over," Leon inquired.

"Congratulation. Finally you got the hang of it," Bill kidded, and though he was miles away and I could only hear his voice that was slightly garbled and sounded high-pitched, I perceived that he was in high spirit. Tony had obviously sensed the same because he transmitted: "You sound chipper. What's the occasion?"

"I'm just feeling good ... that's all," Bill answered, and then asked: "How long will it take you to move and set up?"

"Two days, perhaps three. It depends on what kind
of weather we'll be having up there," Tony replied.

"And you move to Thor, don't you? Seismic 3," Bill
asked, and as I affirmed it, he warned me that Danish
Strait was chocked with rough ice. "You better scout
it by plane," he advised.

"Heard your conversation. I'll send a plane within the next few hours, Seismic 3. Give me your
weather, — over," came over the loudspeaker. It was
our dispatcher in Isachsen.

I thanked him and answered his request about the
weather. After that, radio silence prevailed again.

I could pack up now and move to my next recording
site. It was to be on Thor Island that lies between
Kristoffer Bay and Dome Bay south of Ellef Ringness
Island.

I had packed the instruments and picked up the
geophones when Andrew and Teddy returned. Two seal
carcasses were lashed to the sled.

"Had a good hunt?" I asked.

Teddy nodded and after the usual pause, said: "Bad
storm. Good you say: take tent." His eyes roved
over the immediate surroundings, rested for a moment
on the piles of snow I had removed from inside the
tent, then he looked straight at me and neither his
face nor his voice betraying his feelings, said:
"Think, you much trouble. Me not feel good."

I was thunderstruck. He really cares, I thought and a lump rose in my throat. Hiding my emotion, I said, calmly: "Thanks, Teddy," but did not mention the troubles I had been in. "You guys must be hungry," I said, instead.

"Andrew eat from seal. Me not like," he explained.

This reminded me of having read that the Cree had always shown contempt for their neighbors to the north whose eating habits they had despised and whom they called in their tongue: Askimowew, a term meaning: he eats it raw. I wondered now if what I had read was true and if Teddy felt that way.

"Do you despise Andrew because he eats raw seal meat?" I asked.

He seemed to mull over my question. "What is ... despise?" he asked at length.

"Not like him ... feel that he's bad ... hate him. You understand what I mean?"

There was the usual pause before he said: "No hate him. He no bad. Only eat meat raw. Me cook meat."

Then what I read is a lot of baloney. Or could it be that it was so, but the younger generation doesn't feel that way anymore? This could very well be ..., I stopped because Teddy's "go cook" interrupted my thoughts.

I followed him with my eyes. "What would he think of me if he saw me eat raw liver and relish blubber?"

I muttered, and feeling lighthearted, made up a rhyme
and sang:

> "Seal, creature of the sea,
> You provide the food I like to eat.
> It's thy blubber that makes my fare
> and strengthens me to fight the bear.
> Hail to thee."

Then I went to where Andrew was cutting equal rations from the seal carcasses. The dogs, on their
chain tethers, glowered greedily and licked their
chops in eager anticipation of getting fed.

"Hey, Andrew, give me some blubber ... orkso," I
requested.

He straightened up and smiled.

"You ... Kabluna ... eat blaaber ... good," he
said haltingly, bent down and cut off a piece of blubber. "Ubva!" He handed it to me. (Ubva! means: here
it is!).

"Nakkorami, Inuk," I said, what in English means:
I thank you, man.

Nâmaktok," he replied, and after a pause: "Kabluna."

With my belt knife I cut the piece into small cubes
and put them in my pocket.

He shook his head and asked: "Not eat?"

"I sure will," I replied and put one of the cubes
in my mouth and began to chew it.

"You ... Kabluna ... Inuk," he said and diagonally sliced the air with his right hand.

This was easy for me to understand. As he put it: I was half White and half Eskimo because I ate blubber.

As promised by the dispatcher, the aircraft, piloted by Stu, arrived a few hours later. I recognized Stu's high-pitched voice when he called for the usual information on prevailing barometric pressure, velocity and direction of wind, before attempting to land.

Chuck had told me that Stu was past sixty and one of the old generation bush-pilots. I felt the better for it because flying in this hostile environment was under most circumstances a risky affair, demanding expertise that only experience could provide.

"Where we headin' for?" he asked after I had seated myself in the co-pilot's seat and pulled the seat belt tight.

"Danish Strait. Bill said that it's chocked with ice. I want to see how badly."

"S'pose you're lookin' for a way through, right?"

I affirmed it and folded the topographic map I had brought along to a more manageable size.

"What you say if I'll take her high enough to have a view of the entire jumble, then down to have a close look?" he asked, and as I nodded agreement, he pointed at his earphone and then at my head. I reached behind me and put the set that hung there over my ears.

"Now we don't have to shout," he said over the intercom and began to flick switches and set levers before starting the engine.

Once in the air, I was amazed to see the seemingly endless length and breath of the country that was not touched yet by man's ever-increasing desire to discover and exploit its resources.

The ice condition in the strait were bad, not unlike of what I had seen between Grinnell Peninsula and Table Island — a nightmarish jumble of crushed and tumbled ice. At first sight it appeared to be an impenetrable barrier. But when we flew low over it I saw that it was not all impossible to pass through with our sleds. If Norman and his guys have made it through the mess at Table Island, so will we make it here, I thought, feeling defiant.

"Looks bad, don't it?" Stu interrupted my contemplation.

"Yes. But I'm sure we'll make it through alright," I replied, confident we could cope with whatever we would meet down there.

"Wouldn't it be better and easier to pass over land?" he asked.

I pointed at large patches of bare ground. "We couldn't possibly pull the sleds across them."

"True. I didn't think of that. But how about flying your stuff? Have you thought of that?"

I had. But there were reasons preventing me from
doing it. Firstly, there was no aircraft available
to do it within the next three or four days. Secondly,
if bad weather set in I would be stuck, for how long
nobody could say. But if we traveled on the ice we
could get to our destination even when flying was out.
I told all this to Stu.

"I guess, one must be young and gutsy to do it,"
he said and smiled.

Young I was. Gutsy? I did not consider myself to
be that, but felt that I had to try; that I could not
allow myself to limit my experience by not trying to
do something I had not done before, and only to do
what was considered safe and involved a minimum of
risk.

Experience is never limited and never complete; it
is a collection of events that happens to oneself,
physically and mentally. It is a necessity for going
through life more safely, I thought, and related it
to what I planned to do — to travel through Danish
Strait. And if I fail? Oh well, I'll be blamed for
taking unnecessary chances whether I'll succeed or
not, I concluded.

"Let's fly back to camp," I said to Stu.

From the air the ice appeared an uniform, white

surface with no conspicuous features. And somewhere on this monotonous surface was our camp.

"I'll be damned. Can you see that camp of yours?" Stu asked, shaking his head while he banked the aircraft in a tight turn.

"How did you find it last time?"

"The sun was lower and, remember, you told me where I was when I asked."

"Ask Teddy. He understands English and knows how to use the radio," I suggested.

"You mean the Indian?"

I nodded, and he switched to air-ground communication.

"Seismic 3. Teddy, do you receive?— over," he called, repeating it several times.

A few tense moments passed, then came the answer — a concise: "Yes".

The following verbal exchange with Teddy required much patience, was hilarious to a point, but eventually gave us the clue of where we were relative to the location of our camp. It went like this:

"Teddy, can you see the airplane? — over," Stu asked.

"Wait," Teddy transmitted, and after a long interval came his answer: a simple "yes".

"Teddy, where is it? — over."

"Up there."

Stu smiled. "In which direction? — over."

A long pause prevailed again. Then, "left" was
Teddy's curt reply.

"Now, Teddy, listen good. Do you see the airplane
close to you?"

"No."

Stu switched to intercom. "Have you any sugges-
tion?"

"Let me talk to him," I replied, and when he had
switched back to air-ground, I asked: "Teddy, is the
airplane coming toward you or going away from you?"

Stu nodded, and I could read "good' from his lips.

There was a prolonged pause. Then Teddy said:
"Go."

My nerves began to tingle. Don't get impatient,
my inner voice reminded. Just keep asking.

"Teddy, from which side of the tent is the airplane going away?"

"Your place," was his immediate, but curt answer.

"Teddy, stand by," I said, and motioned for Stu to
switch to intercom. "The camp's north of us. You
heard him. He said: your place, and this means: my
cot which is on the south side of the tent," I explained, then added, kiddingly: "At least it was
there when we left."

Stu's eyes sparkled. "I hope you're right," he
said, and flew a tight turn. Before he had leveled

the wings we shouted in unison: "There it is!"

The camp had popped in sight as if out of nowhere.
I asked him why he had not seen it before.

"Hard to say," he replied, let the flaps out,
throttled the engine, and shortly after we touched
down. I exhaled with relief.

Teddy told us that we had flown twice past the
camp. "Me think what you do? Then hear radio."

Stu praised him for his assistance, and though
Teddy's face remained expressionless, I could see
that he was pleased.

"Coffee?" he asked, and as Stu nodded, he poured
two cups, then left the tent.

"He don't talk much, that's for sure," Stu remarked, and took a sip. "But he makes good coffee,"
he added, took another sip, and setting down the cup,
seemed to get lost in thoughts.

At length, as if talking to himself, he said:
"I'd taken a bearing on those hills north of here and
knew I was on course, just couldn't see no camp. Was
that cursed flat light. I've seen it before. Really
plays tricks on a guy."

He looked at me. "You sure knew how to talk to
him. You're a cool one," he said.

"Not as cool as you think," I replied, then told
him that I had worried we would not find the camp
again. And that I had realized it would be extremely

difficult to find someone who was on the ice and needed assistance, but had no radio or any means of making his whereabout visible to the pilot.

"You're so right," he said, musingly, and I wondered whether he had experienced such case or cases.

"Have you ever ...." I started to ask, then stopped speaking because Teddy parted the entrance flaps
of the tent and said: "Come look."

The thought of bear shot through my head, and without a moment's hesitation I rushed outside. There was
no bear. But dogs had raided our food cache. They
had made off with all sausages, most of the meat, and
much of the rice, cereals and dried fruit was spilled.

"How could this happen?" I cried, furious and dis-
gusted.

Teddy's eyes were downcast. "Andrew ... me ... in
tent. Dogs break rope ... eat meat ... run away ...
we not hear," he said, softly, then added: "Me sorry."

My anger spent, I said: "Don't blame yourself. It
wasn't your mistake that the dogs got loose."

Stu had joined us. "What a mess," he remarked,
shaking his head.

"It's not the first time they've done it," I said,
and a thought struck me. "Would you have time to fly
to Table Island? There's some food I left behind."

"Let's see," he drawled, mumbled a few words while
counting them off on his fingers, looked up at the sky,

checked his watch, took a few steps back and forth, then said, decidedly: "Why not! An hour more or less won't matter."

And I was glad for that.

It was perhaps an hour later when the aircraft's skis made contact with the snow and instantly sank deep. The forward motion stopped abruptly — the aircraft was stuck in one of the many snowdrifts the recent blizzard had left behind.

"Damn! It just grabbed and pulled in," Stu exclaimed, flicking switches. "I should have known and stayed over there," he went on and pointed to a wind-blown ridge.

For a very long time we shoveled snow. A brisk wind was blowing, making it a miserable affair. After we had freed the aircraft I went in search of the cache. It was buried under a huge snowdrift, and only because a foot or two of bamboo pole stuck out of it did I find it. Digging it out, I found that wolves and foxes had raided it and none of the food was left.

Heck, with the generator, I thought vexed, and decided to leave it behind because it was under more hard-packed snow, and I was loath to do more shoveling.

In the meantime Stu had taxied the aircraft to the ridge and had run up the engine for takeoff.

"No supplies?" he declared as I climbed into the cockpit and stammered my discovery. "Now don't feel bad about coming here for nothing. Mainthing, we didn't wreck the plane," he consoled.

His eyes roved over the instruments, his hands were on the throttle and the steering.

"Pump the skis all the way up. We don't need 'em here," he said. A light danced in his eyes. "It's kind of rough ... the ground, I mean. So hang on," he added, and pushed the throttle forward.

And it was rough. The aircraft swayed and bounced and jerked while gathering speed. Scared out of my wits I thought my early demise was rapidly approaching, and not before the wheels broke contact with the ground and the aircraft climbed into the sky did I relax and look down to where the tracks of our toil were being wiped out by drifting snow.

CHAPTER 7

It was a rather pleasant day with a cloudless, blue
sky and a light breeze that drifted snow in small
whisks across the vast expanse of the frozen sea.
Heat waves glimmered, and through them mirages of fan-
tastic forms and extent played their magic.

The dogs trotted at a steady pace, pulling the
heavily loaded kamotik. Teddy, pulling the even
heavier loaded 'Nansen' sled with the snowmobile,
followed our tracks at a distance.

The sun stood low on the horizon when we passed
the first, scattered patches of jumbled ice. The sky
began to overcast, the breeze stopped blowing, the
air did no more glimmer, the mirages disappeared.

Andrew stopped the dogs, and Teddy caught up. We
squatted about our supper table — part of a crate —
ate frozen sardines and tunafish, pilot biscuits, and
drank mugful after mugful of bitter-tasting tea.

Then we headed for what appeared the only gap in
an otherwise uninterrupted barricade of jumbled ice.
Again, Andrew led the way, guiding the dogs with his
guttural chant of orders. I sat on the sled and
watched the dogs toil at their traces. And I listened to the din of the snowmobile that swelled, then
waned, and sometimes died out all together, only to
come on loud again, assuring me that Teddy was

following us, though often out of sight. And I looked with apprehension at the unearthly scenery of mis-
shapen forms of ice which loomed and seemed to glower
benumbed all about us.

We followed an old, frozen lead. Flat and smooth,
the width of about ten yards, it led in a zigzag
course through the crushed and piled up jumble. It
was easy going, and it could have deceived me had I
not known that this frozen rent led but a short distance into the ice pack and was coming to an end long
before we would reach smooth ice surface again.

Having reached the lead's end, an exhausting struggled began for us and the dogs. We encountered everything that can make sledging an almost impossible affair. Huge chunks of ice surrounded us. Some were
part of long snowdrifts, others were swept clear by
wind. The spaces between these chunks were filled-in
with snow, soft and waist-deep in places, hard-packed
and studded with crushed pieces of ice in others.
Ridges of broken, rafted ice ran like fences in all
directions.

The dogs lurched and strained, floundered, pawed,
yelped and whined. Andrew and I pushed and pulled to
help the dogs. We slipped and stumbled, cursed and
laughed, and only paused long enough to stop panting.

Though we progressed at a slow pace, Teddy could
not keep up with us. The snowmobile got stuck in

loose snow, spun out on hard surface, was difficult, almost impossible, to steer in tight spots, and many times we had to pull his sled with the dogs.

It was grueling labor for man and beast, and when our advance slowed to near standstill we made camp. Andrew cared for the dogs, Teddy pitched a tent, while I prepared a hot meal, right in the open. Then we sacked out.

Refreshed by several hours sleep we broke camp and after a filling meal continued our journey. Patches of fog lay over the ice; scattered clouds hung in the sky, and the sun blazed intermittently through them. The air was warm and humid. The snow had turned soft, almost mushy.

We struggled on. The sleds rose and plunged, slipped sideways or ran down-slope, burying their fronts in soft snowdrifts or crushing them into piled up ice. And when it seemed that we had come through the worst, it was but the beginning of worse conditions. Our physical endurance was taxed to its very limit.

At long last the field of upheaved ice was behind us and we could gaze at the flat expanse of Kristoffer Bay.

We had made it through the strait!

To cross that stretch of pack ice, which I had estimated to be about twenty miles long, had taken us almost two days. I was convinced that had we a second

186

team of dogs instead of a snowmobile, we could have
done it in less time and with less struggle. I felt
that traveling with dogs was easier and safer than
having to rely on a snowmobile, especially then when
one could not count on being supplied by aircraft at
regular intervals or when one encountered dangerous
ice conditions.

Thor Island was still thirty miles distant. Since
Kristoffer Bay was smooth ice with the exception of a
few pressure ridges and small patches of pack ice, I
figured we would arrive there within a few hours.
But we hit an open lead of about fifteen feet width,
a jagged rent too wide for us to cross. It ran in
southwesterly direction across the bay and almost at
right angle to our course. Out of the dark water
popped up a few ringed seal, stared shortly at us,
then sank noiselessly back into the icy reaches. Seeing this , sent shivers through my body.

To cross over we had to find a narrow or the end
of the lead. Luck or whatever it may be called was
with us, for within a mile or so we found a sort of a
bridge — a few small floes jammed together.

Without any preliminaries Andrew ran across it.
And he made it without wetting his kamiks. This en-
ticed me to follow him. I stepped on the nearest
floe, felt the sickening motion of sinking, and rushed ahead mindless of where I stepped.

Andrew watched me. "Very good," he said. Then he
ran back to fetch the dogs and sled. But the dogs
groveled and whimpered, and not before he used the
whip did they obey his command. Then they passed so
fast across the floes that neither they nor the sled
had time to sink.

Now that Teddy could not do the same with the snowmobile because it was too heavy and cumbersome to
make it safely, he had no other choice than to follow
the lead which might stretch all the way to the shore,
about three miles distant.

Andrew and I sledged on. Through my binoculars I
saw Teddy drive onto shore which was littered with
grounded ice, and within seconds he disappeared behind it.

Minutes passed. He did not re-appear. Andrew
halted the dogs — we waited. As more time passed
without Teddy re-appearing, apprehension gripped me
and I decided to go and find out what held him up.

"Andrew, you stay here," I said and pointed downward.

He understood , seated himself on the sled and began to smoke a cigarette. To sledge there was an unnecessary strain on the dogs.

I was about halfway to the shore when a breeze
sprang up and a wall resembling white cotton approached me — I was in fog.

The sudden transition was startling. I had been in sunshine with a cloud-studded sky above me and now, as an instance leaps, the sun was blotted out, there was no more sky, and I felt as if a wet veil had descended upon me. It was weird, but also frightening. For all I could make out I might as well have been suspended in space. Turning around, I could not see the tracks I had left in the snow. There was no horizon. The thought of polar bear scared me. I listened intently, and stared into the fog. My heart pounded, I breathed with difficulty, and I could see nothing but white. I did not dare to move for fear of falling over obstacles or stepping into a hole or crack.

Recalling the conditions Andrew and I had been trapped in, I concluded that I had to wait patiently for a pending change; that the fog would lift or dissolve, sooner or later. But this did not prevent my mind from conjuring up pictures of perils I had never thought of before. I did not discover in me the calmness required to remain at ease as Andrew had been. It was the difference between two temperaments — one stoic, the other passionate.

The spooky condition seemed to last forever. And then, all of a sudden, I heard the faint noise of a running engine. I wanted to shout, but did not dare for fear of bears. Instead, I shuffled in direction of the noise.

The breeze grew strong and sight returned. I saw
sky, and like an actor stepping from the dim, curtain-
shrouded backstage into the dazzling light of the
stage, I stepped into the arctic landscape.

I was very near the shore bordered by a gigantic
maze of grounded ice that made me feel dwarf-like, a
brother to Tom Thumb. And in this bewildering barricade struggled Teddy with snowmobile and sled. He
seemed as much surprised as glad when I caught up
with him. The snow was soft, mushy, and not before
we had left the last of the towering chunks of ice
behind us was the going easy.

With the exception of the few pressure ridges and
patches of rough ice, which we crossed with relative
ease, the rest of the way was smooth ice.

This should have made sledging enjoyable. But a
raw, gusty wind, driving snow, sleet and hail, made
it a miserable affair. I was amazed to see the
change the warm weather had wrought on land. The snow
cover had but disappeared, and only in gullies between bare sand and gravel bars lay it still deep and
soft. Where scant vegetation clung to soil, the top-
most layer was sodden.

Following a wide gully, we headed inland for a
stretch, then pitched camp and, without eating or
drinking anything, hit the sack. We had not slept in

more than forty hours.

The roar of engines, screaming gears and the clatter of steel tracks woke me. The Shooting Crew had arrived and — George. No sooner had I put pants and shirt on and was lacing my mukluks, stood he in front of me and yelled: "You, you ... don't you have enough sense to put up the radio!"

Without letting me explain why I had not done it yet, he called me irresponsible, yelled: that since three hours a loaded airplane was standing-by at Isachsen, waiting for my weather report without which the pilot would not take off; that I was holding up the entire operation.

I tried again to explain, but he did not listen, cursed me instead for laziness and that he was fed up with my stupidity. His tongue-lashing was decidedly not funny, and only with the utmost effort could I constrain myself not to lose my temper and return like for like. Half through his dressing me down the tent flaps parted and Norman stepped in. For a few moments he listened to George's raving, then laid a hand on his shoulder and said: "Can't you understand that these guys needed a rest after what they've been through? Not all are Superman like you seem to be."

George gulped. With a violent move he shook off Norman's hand, turned on his heels and stormed out of the tent.

Norman grinned. "Don't take it hard. He's just upset that you didn't answer his calls. He'll simmer down as usual."

"I know it's my mistake. But we were so dogtired I did not bother ...,"

"There's no problem," he interrupted. "Dale's bringing powder, that's all. And we can wait for that." He smiled and added: "We also need a rest."

He turned to leave, then faced me again. "You went through that piled up mess that's plugging the strait?" he asked with a tone of admiration in his voice.

"Yes. There was no other way!" I blurted out. "Huge chunks ... pressure ridges ... soft snow ... dogs is the answer ... hopeless with snowmobiles," I babbled away, trying to tell the whole story in one burst of words.

He nodded, musingly. "Remember? I know how it is."

He gave a nod in the direction George had gone. "But he sure doesn't like what you did. Said: you jeopardized the whole outfit of yours."

I felt my cheeks redden. "I knew he would say that. But how else could I have come here? By plane? There was none available, and I didn't trust the weather to hold till one was free."

"If I were you I wouldn't worry," he returned and left.

Some time later Teddy and I set up the masts,
strung the antenna between them and connected it to
the radio. Then I got in contact with Isachsen. By
that time the sky was overcast and progressively dark-
ening to a leaden gray toward the west where the sun
showed as a faint yellow dot. The threat of a blizzard lay over the land.

"How long till it begins to blow at your place?"
the dispatcher asked after I had told him all that.

"I'd say a few hours, — over."

"Good enough. Stand by. I'll let you know if
Dale wants to risk it."

A few minutes passed before he reported that M-E-S
would be on the way. I felt greatly relieved because
that would mollify George, and he would perhaps realize that I had not messed up the operation, as he had
said. We would get explosives. Food and fuel? That
was something nobody seemed to know, and I hoped that
the storm would hold off long enough for Dale to make
a second trip should there be no food and fuel on
board this time. Isachsen was a mere forty miles
distant.

But the sequence of events did not turn out as I
had wished for. Dale brought the explosives alright,
but then the blizzard came earlier than I had figured,
blew during a day and a half, leaving in its wake a
blanket of snow. And only then did we get food and

fuel. It was Dale who brought them. He used the skis to land the aircraft, for the blanket of snow hid the contour of the ground.

"It sure was rough. Hit a few rocks," he remarked.

After he had checked the skis for possible damage — "A few more scratches, that's all," he said — we had coffee.

He told me that Stu's and Chuck's airplanes were already changed to big tires; that big tires allowed to land and take off where the normal, small wheels would not; that he would fly south to have his plane prepared for summer operation, and that he would take some time off work.

"I haven't had a break in a long time," he said, and then added: "So, I won't fly for you no more, I guess."

I walked with him to the aircraft.

"Take care. It was just great flying for you," he said with a smile, climbed into the cockpit and then took off.

As he flew over the camp and dipped the wings in parting, I waved good-bye. I had appreciated his skill in flying in this treacherous arctic land.

Teddy and I were laying out the recording spread as the Shooting Crew left. When the unit Leon was driving passed us, Edgar leaned out of its cab and called with a big grin on his face: "Hurry up, you guys, or we'll be ready before you are!"

"You make bet?" Teddy shouted.

Edgar shook his head, and we could see his lips
move, but did not understand what he said, for the
noise of the running gears and tracks drowned out his
voice.

Norman and Mike had left hours earlier — they were
surveying line. George followed the Shooting Crew.

"I'll be back!" he shouted as he passed us.

We were on good terms again.

"I didn't mean to shout at you. But there's so
much on my mind, and I'm constantly worrying about
the outcome of the survey, that I lose my temper sometimes," he had said to me, and then added what I had
never expected him to say: "I know that I'm in the
wrong sometimes."

This statement changed my opinion of him to the
better, and I promised myself to be more tolerant myself.

The weather was unstable. The sun shone brightly
for a while, the snow dazzled, melted, then clouds
scudded across the country, followed by flurries.
The temperature fell, the snow hardened, the melting
stopped. Back was the sun, the dazzle, the snow
thawed again.

Laying out the recording spread was routine now,
and it was not long before I could report via radio

195

that I was ready to record. An hour or so later Leon
exploded the first shot for the new location, and
during the following day several more, all of which I
recorded without encountering problems with the instruments of the geophones.

So George would have his own quater when he returned, Teddy pitched the pyramid tent that was an
item of our emergency gear. Then he left with Andrew
to hunt seal.

I read for a while and then turned in. It seemed
I had not slept long when I awoke sensing that I was
in imminent danger. The moment I opened my eyes my
heart leapt in terror, for a polar bear cub stood beside my cot and from the outside I heard a low growl,
the call of mother bear. I saw her silhouetted
against the canvas of the tent.

The cub bawled, mother answered, and up came her
front paws — right over my cot. Fast as lightning,
I was out of the sleeping bag and grabbed the rifle
that lay beside me on the floor. Frightened by my
actions the cub drew back and wailed.

"Stop that! You little beast! Go to mama!" I
cried, annoyed, not thinking of the consequences.

The cub drew farther back and bawled terrified.
And outside mother growled louder, reared up and
dealt the tent a swat. The frame squeaked and gave a
little. I swung the rifle and hit her with its butt

in the rump. She roared enraged, dropped on all four, moved a few feet down the tent — I saw it all through the canvas — and with another swat rent the wall. As chance had it, it was where an upper cross-pipe of the frame was missing.

There she stood halfway across the lower cross-pipe, her jaws agape, her beady eyes fixed on me, not more than five feet from where I kneeled on my cot. It was the confrontation I had dreaded most. She lifted her paw — slowly, it seemed to me.

She'll kill me! flashed through my head.

I flipped the rifle, flicked the safety catch and pulled the trigger. The bullet — it was a 220 grain slug — knocked her back, she dropped, a convulsion ran through her body, then she lay lifeless.

Whirling around, I saw that the cub had left the tent. My mind blank, my heart pounding, I dressed myself with trembling hands, then left the tent. And what I saw wrung my heart — the little bear wailed and nudged its mother, pleading for a sign of recognition. I felt awful!

After I had regained some measure of composure I tried to catch the cub. It reared up and snarled and dodged all my attempts to grab it. After a while I gave up and, instead, back-tracked the spoor the bears had left. What the spoor revealed was a drama played on nature's stage by creatures who must hunt for their survival.

The she-bear had ambled with two small offsprings in a zigzagging course from hummock to hummock, digging here, sniffing there. Then four wolves had shown up and attacked — I made out four different paw sizes. The much trampled, blood-splattered snow showed that the ensuing battle had been vicious; that one cub was killed and carried off by the wolves.

She had lain down for a while — a patch of snow was glazed from her body heat — and then continued her search for food.

From about a mile distance she had winded our camp and had headed straight for it. Arriving where the dogs had been tethered and fed, she had nosed about and then, bypassing Andrew's tent, had made for the pyramid tent. Big smudges on its white canvas showed that she had pawed but not damaged it. Circling it, she had come to my tent where I had lain asleep. I had not tied the entrance flaps, and so the cub had walked straight in. Had she followed it, I would not have had a chance to save myself!

Standing at the site where the battle between bear and wolves had taken place, the thought struck me that after the wolves had devoured the cub they might have trailed their foe with her remaining cub.

Alarmed, I ran back to camp, but was too late: the wolves had been there. Their tracks were all about

the place, and I found the spot where they had cor-
nered and killed the cub, then made off with it.

Depressed, I sat on a box and looked at the she-
bear who lay dead beside the tent. Even though I had
killed her in self-defense, I felt bad about it. It
was a sentiment I had not discovered in Andrew. He
was proud at having killed bears, adults and young
ones, apparently for no other reason than to get their
skins and meat for the dogs, the latter, I suspected,
not having been his prime consideration.

If the bear wouldn't have met me, and I would not
have had to kill her, could she have saved her remaining cub from the wolves? I asked myself, and concluded
that her chances to do so would have been minimal.

Then why do I feel bad? I kept asking myself. Is
it not in the order of things: survival at the cost
of others! But even that reflection did not set me
at ease. I still wished I would not have had to kill
her.

Hours later Andrew and Teddy returned. They had
bagged a seal. Though they did not utter more than a
few words of amazement when they surveyed the damage
the bear had done to the tent, and how close it was
to my cot, it seemed that my deed earned their admiration.

The bear was so heavy that even three strong we had
to strain hard to move it some distance from the tent

where Andrew skinned it and cut up for dog feed.

I sewed the rent in the tent wall while Teddy prepared a meal. All was back to normal, and when
George returned — as he had said he would — only an
observant eye would have discovered traces of the incident. He missed the traces, and I had no reason to
tell him.

Nevertheless, he was pleased to have his own quarter now. After he had eaten the pork chops and flap-
jacks Teddy had cooked for him, he told me that he
wanted to take a bath.

"Where would you like to take it ... and may we
watch?" I kidded.

He called me a silly so-and-so, and said he would
take it in his tent.

"You have a spare stove to melt snow, don't you?"
he asked.

"A spare stove? You must be joking!" I retorted.

He flinched as if he had been slapped, and I knew
that I had driven my point home because several times
I had asked him for permission to order a spare stove,
but he had always refused to give it.

"Then have Teddy set up the one you have in my
tent while I service the snowmobile," he requested.

"It's not your tent, and you must pay rent for it,"
I funned.

He laughed and shook his head. "Has the Arctic

affected your brain or are you naturally greedy?" he
returned good-humored.

I was checking seismic records as I heard him yell:
"Fire! Help! Fire!"

I gasped. Fire spelled disaster! I snatched up
the fire extinguisher, which stood near the entrance
of the tent — I had made it a rule to always place it
there — and rushed outside to see the pyramid tent
afire. Flames shot through its vent and out of the
rolled-up sleeve entrance through which George had
burst into the open.

"The stove exploded," he stammered and clutched my
arm.

"Let me go!" I yelled, tore myself free, rushed up
to the tent and sprayed through the entrance its blaz-
ing interior. The flames collapsed, and steam vented.

I could see no damage to the tent.

"So the stove exploded?" I mocked, then shouted:
"That's nonsense! And you know it! You were care-
less!"

"You have no right to say that," he demurred. "I
only refilled the pot with snow ...,"

"And didn't wipe its bottom before you set it back
onto the burner," I interrupted him.

His face reddened. I knew I was right. Snow
clinging to the bottom of the pot, had killed the
flame, and as he had tried to re-light it, the fuel

that had flowed from the pressurized tank over the
stove and possibly part of the ground sheet had igni-
ted explosion-like. It could have cost the tent, if
not set the entire camp afire.

For once, he seemed disconcerted. "I'm leaving so
you won't have to be afraid that I burn down your
camp," he said.

"Now you're talking nonsense," I declared and
pointed out that the weather was rapidly detoriorat-
ing; that no man in his right mind would travel alone
at a time like this, and that he should stay.

"You still can have your bath," I tempted.

Whether the mishap had bruised his ego or whether
he suddenly had changed his plans, as he quite often
did, he did not heed my advice, packed up his things
and left.

Teddy and Andrew were playing cards. The commotion
brought them outside. Both overheard my warning about
the weather.

"Him crazy ... go into storm," Teddy remarked.

"Boss ... tukikangitok," said Andrew.

"Tuki ... what?" I asked, trying to pronounce the
word.

He repeated it until I got it right. Now that I
could pronounce it I still did not know what it meant.
So I raised my shoulder and holding the shrug, indicated to him that its meaning was lost to me.

He tapped his temple. "No good," he said.

I figured that tukikangitok meant the same as Teddy had implied: George was a fool to go into a storm.

(Later, I asked Edgar about the proper meaning of that word. "It means: has no sense," he said).

Teddy cleaned up the inner of the pyramid tent. As I had guessed, there was no damage to it. I was certain now that I had not unjustly accused George of carelessness.

It had been another incident that could have had disastrous consequences, and I wondered whether my luck would run out, and if so, when and how.

Sometime later a southwesterly wind brought low-lying clouds. The surroundings obscured and snow began to fall. And somewhere out there, exposed to this bitter weather, was George trying to find his way back to our camp. He had transmitted by radio that he had lost the tracks of the Shooting Crew, did not know where he was and was turning back. To go and meet him was too risky for anyone because visibility was almost zero. Therefore, we stayed put.

"Call me in an hour again. I'm standing by," I requested.

"Will do, — over and out," was his answer.

The hour passed. But he did not call. I waited ten minutes, then sent my inquiry about the weather he was in, and whether he knew how close he was to

our camp. The loudspeaker boomed in reply. Yet it
was not George who called, but Bill. He was, like me,
concerned about George's whereabout.

"What can we do? — over," I asked.

"In this weather? Nothing! Just wait and hope
that he's all right, — over and standing by."

I waited again, transmitted from time to time in-
quiries addressed to George, and hoped to receive his
reply that he was all right and would be in camp,
shortly. I also left the tent to stand in the open
and to listen if I could hear the din of the snowmobile or shouts. It was to no avail. Silence prevailed. And to make matters worse, radio blackout
occurred.

Three quarter of a day passed before snow stopped
falling and a brisk wind cleared the sky. The sun
warmed the air again; the surroundings sparkled,
blinding the eye. Radio communication restored.

The dispatcher at Isachsen asked for the weather
report.

"Your boss wants to fly down to your place, —
over," he added.

"What? He's with you? — over."

"Affirmative. He arrived here an hour ago, — over."

Anger gripped me. "May I talk with him?" I requested.

"He's resting now. But I'll tell him to contact

you, — over."

"Thanks. Standing by."

That jackass! That fink! has left me in the air
about his change of mind and caused me all the anxiety that he might be in grave danger! I went on to
myself. This sentiment was confirmed by Bill.

"He's an inconsiderate SOB, that's all there is to
it, — over," he transmitted.

George did not radio, but five hours later arrived
by aircraft piloted by Chuck who, except for saying:
"Howdy", did not talk and took to the sky again right
after we had unloaded the explosives he had on board.
I felt that there was tension between the two, and
most likely the cause for his uncommunicative behavior.

George stayed. I was no longer angry, but rather
glad that he was safe and had suffered no injury. But
I wanted to know what had happened. His story was
one of daring, perhaps too much of it, for his action
could have ended in tragedy, not only involving him,
but others, too.

Shortly after his radio message that he would turn
around, his snowmobile had broken down. Figuring the
time and speed he had been traveling, he became convinced that he had crossed Noice Peninsula. Thus he
decided to walk straight north. He would reach
Isachsen, sooner or later.

"I figured that it was closer to go there than return to your camp," he said.

"Then you always knew where you were!" I burst out,
anger rising in me again.

"Not exactly," he responded. "Anyway, to make a
long story short, I found it, didn't I?" he concluded
with a grin while he stroked his stubbled chin and
cheeks.

"For heaven's sake, why didn't you let me know that
you changed your mind and went to Isachsen?" I demanded.

He looked me straight in the eyes, and said: "To be
honest, it never occurred to me to do that. It wasn't
important anyway."

"Damn you! Can't you get it into your thick scull
that we worried?" I exploded.

He smirked. "Now were you really?"

"Oh, go to hell!" I barked, turned around and left
the tent.

I was irritated that he scoffed at anyone's concern
about his welfare. And still I felt a vague admiration for his exploits. In spite of all the contro-
versies and conflicts that took place among us, I har-
bored no enmity toward him. He had done me no harm.
We had disagreements about the way of doing things.
It was not that I did not accept suggestions from him
if they proved to better my methods of doing things,
or that I did not listen to and to value his profes-

206

sional experience in seismic recording and interpretation. No! It was his abrupt, often contemptuous, manner that irritated me, and others too, I had observed.

All of us had the same motivation: we wanted to succeed in what we had set out to do — a scientific survey that would prove of value, and contribute to the knowledge of the area's geologic formation that lay thousands of feet under ice-covered water. And that, I felt, was worth all the physical and mental hardship each of us was confronted with, and underwent at times.

It was now the eight of June. The spring-like weather had backed toward winter. A blizzard howled and plastered the landscape and our camp with sleet that froze in bizarre forms to boxes, masts, guys and tents. It lasted throughout the day, and when I reported the prevailing weather to Isachsen in the evening, the wind was still gusting with the strength that threatened to tear the guy ropes of tents and masts from their pegs — to lay waste our camp. But later, as sudden as the storm had hit as sudden it also passed, and back was the breakup atmosphere.

George assembled and checked equipment. He wanted to blast the few remaining shot points by himself.

"To try out new blasting procedures which have been on my mind since the beginning of the survey," he told me. What they were he kept secret.

He commandeered Andrew and Teddy to help him with
the drilling and the loading of the shot points. The
two men had planned to go hunting seal, and if a
chance would present itself, to bag a bear. Though
both remained silent, I saw that they were disappointed. I had learned to read slight nuances in
their facial expressions — they did no longer appear
to me completely stoical.

After the three had left I went to check out the
recording spread to make sure that no bear or wolf or
fox had played with geophones, chewed the cables or
made off with some of either. All these things had
happened before, necessitating hours of repair work.

Not only these animals created problems, the
weather did too. And the ones caused by it were more
difficult to find: ice formed between contacts,
broken cables, loose contacts, shifted geophone
plants and more.

Now I plodded through deep snowdrifts, sank into
slush up to my knees, slithered over melting ground,
dug, scraped and cleaned, twisted broken wires and
insulated them with tape. By the time the spread was
checked out and was ready so that I could record
without encountering dead traces, my mukluks and mittens were soaked, my feet and hands frozen, and my
outer garment was wet and splattered with mud.

I had no insulated rubber boots — they were in the cache at Table Island. I was paying now for inexperience as any man will at one time or another. It was a lesson I always remembered thereafter, and never again left I footwear or clothing behind, even though I did not wear them at the time.

After another day and a half of recording, the program was completed.

"Guys, we did it! It's just great! I'm going to pack up now and leave this godforsaken place as soon as I can get an airplane," Tony commented from his station at Cape Isachsen on the north coast of Ellef Ringness Island. "See you guys in Isachsen," he added.

"So will I," responded Bill from his station on King Christian Island.

"Don't forget to fetch me," I reminded.

"Don't worry, we won't leave you out there," Tony commented.

"I thought you'd like to stay for the summer," taunted Bill.

George did not join in these lighthearted exchange. His only comment was: "Did each of you get the last shot all right?"

And that we had!

I packed the instruments, then went to pick up the recording spread.

"For the last time," I said out loud .

CHAPTER 8

During the past two days it had been sunny and warm
— two to three degrees above freezing. Had spring arrived? It seemed so until the sky overcast, a cold
wind began to blow, and flurries scudded across land
and ice — wintry climate had returned. It brought
with it an unexpected problem: heated by the sun's ra-
diation during the past days, the black, rubber-coated
recording cable had melted into the ice and where it
lay on land into the upper layer of soil. Now, the
weather having backed up to winter, it froze in over
long stretches. This forced me to chip it out with an
ice pick, then rub off the lumps of soil that clung to
it before I could wind it onto its reels. It was no
easy job, and for hours I toiled with dogged determination.

Hours later George and Teddy returned, but not
Andrew. When I asked where he was, George shrugged
his shoulder, whereas Teddy said: "Me think ... Andrew
go kill seal for dog."

I figured that he was right.

George told me that he and Teddy were going to help
Bill move his stuff from his present station on King
Christian Island to Isachsen, and that this would take
several days.

"How about me and my things?" I asked.

"You'll just have to wait till it's your turn to be picked up, that's all," he said with a grin.

This made me feel as if I was something of no more use to him.

"I'm amazed how kind you are. A real nice guy," I returned, sarcastically.

"Thank you," he said, rather cordially, and I was not sure whether he had gotten the drift of what I had implied, or whether he made light of it.

After we had eaten the meal I cooked he called the dispatcher at Isachsen. And a few hours later Stu arrived with his aircraft and flew him and Teddy to Bill's camp.

Alone again, I packed up the pyramid tent and all equipment I did use no more.

The weather remained moody. For hours a ghostly calm prevailed during which the fog was so thick I could not see anything beyond ten paces. Then wind sprung up, the fog dissolved, the sun shone brightly from a cloudless sky, the temperature of the air rose to forty degrees Fahrenheit. Snow and ice melted, water ran all over, the land softened and became muddy. These conditions lasted a few hours, then fog drifted in again, shrouding the country in mystery, and snow flurries drove across the tundra, dusting it white.

A day passed and another while I waited for Andrew

to return.

'It's getting muddier with every passing hour. The snow has gone except in the gully that runs past the camp down to the ice. If Andrew doesn't arrive soon, his dogs won't be able to pull the kamotik farther than the shore, and we have to pack every-thing up to the camp.' I wrote in my diary. Next day I wrote: 'There's no more kerosine for the heater. It's damp and cold, and if I'm not walk-ing about, I freeze. Even the sleeping bag is damp and does not feel warm anymore. I wish the weather would improve and the sun would shine. It's almost raining now. I feel miserable.'

Wind rose the following night. It moaned first, then changed its tune to a steady whistling, and at four o'clock in the morning hail pattered the canvas of the tent.

I crawled out of the sleeping bag, dressed and went outside. The hail changed to wind-driven rain drops. They wetted my face. I tilted my head back, opened my mouth and swallowed the drops that fell into it. It was a welcome sensation — rain instead of snow — and it dispelled my listlessness. I went back inside and began to read.

Once in a while I put the book aside and listened to the raindrops drumming fitfully on the canvas. And then, shortly before noon, I heard dogs yelp and pant, and the grating of sled runners.

Andrew had returned! And I was glad to have company.

Two seal carcasses were strapped onto the sled.

"No nanuk?" I asked.

He shook his head and smiled, but did not offer any explanation.

After he had cared for the dogs and unloaded the sled he went to sleep in his tent, and not before late afternoon of the following day did he wake up. He had slept well over sixteen hours. Although both of us had the physical condition to stay awake for days on end, I could never match his ability to sleep that long. Compared to him I was an insomniac.

While he slept, two dogs freed themselves of their tether, broke into my meat cache, gorged down the remaining pork chops and made off with the last of the sausages. They did not feed on the seal carcasses. This surprised and puzzled me, but did not prevent me from chasing the thieves. I caught one and gave him such sound thrashing that he broke into a crescendo of wails. Then I dragged the whimpering creature to its place, secured it to its tether and after giving it a last kick, more to emphasize a command than handing out additional punishment, turned away.

What happened moments later I reckoned to be an act of showing contempt or perhaps a lecture in

do-not-get-caught-next-time. It also could have been
a part of dog justice. The leader of the team pounced
on the still whimpering mate, caught him by the scruff
of the neck and shook him. Then, the hairs along his
back standing erect, his tail stretched out, he stood,
snarling viciously, over the pitifully crying under-
ling who groveled, turned on his back exposing his
throat to the threatening fangs of his master. This
pose of boss and subordinate lasted till there seemed
to be total submission on part of the one and undis-
puted dominance on part of the other. Then 'Scarface'
returned to his own place. I had given the lead-dog
this name because an ugly scar stretched across his
muzzle, the mark of a previous fight, possibly for
dominance.

He had also freed himself of his tether, but had
neither partaken in the raid nor had he strayed. He
displayed the character of a true leader who does not
indulge himself in personal likings, but acts as a
model.

I caught myself thinking of the dogs as I would
think of people — I was perhaps idiolizing the beast.
And that, at close scrutiny, I discovered to be the
result of having lived in the wild over long periods
of time. Yet, considering the dogs, there was no
doubt in my mind that these creatures formed a commu-
nity in which each member had a distinct status.

214

Whether this status was the result of the individual dog's physical makeup or mental capacity or a combination of both I could not figure out. One thing I was sure of however: majority did not rule — superior strength and cunning was law. There was number one, then two, then tree, and so on to the last, poor mutt who was the best example of a real underdog, despised and often mistreated by its mates. I had observed this since the day Andrew had joined me with his team of dogs at Table Island.

I was hungry, but the thought of eating revolted me, for there was nothing else left in the boxes than a few cans of sardines and tuna fish, a package of hardtack and several handfuls of raisins. I had no coffee, only tea. Sugar and powdered milk were gone, and canned milk I had not seen in weeks.

I drank the tea without sugar. It tasted bitter and was not to my liking. Sardines or tuna fish I mixed with small bits of raw blubber or raisins just to vary their taste. One must have lived on a diet that invariably tastes the same to discover what ghastly trouble the necessity of swallowing one's food may become. Then, and only then, one might understand that such concoctions appear appetizing, at least for a time.

Andrew did not mix the food. He ate the sardines and tuna fish and blubber separately, and he wrinkled

his nose and shook his head while he watched me chew
the mixtures.

It continued to rain, varying between downpours and
drizzle. The snow had melted, the ground continued
thawing and turned temporarily to mud, deep and sticky.

A day later, when Chuck circled over the camp, trying to find a firmed-up strip of terrain on which to
land his aircraft, I was tempted to let him do it. He
was flying from King Christian Island back to Isachsen
and had announced over the VHF radio that we was coming in because he had room for me and some gear.

But common sense won the upper hand in me. A landing was just too risky — the aircraft might become
stuck in deep mud. What's another few days? We'll
survive, won't we? my inner voice whispered, half-
heartedly.

"You'll get stuck if you'll try it. It's too soft,
— over," I transmitted.

"Thanks for telling me. Let me know when it's
dried up a bit," Chuck responded, and then added: "I
saw a few musk-oxen south of your camp, — over."

I heard the engine increase its roar — the aircraft
was climbing out of sight.

"Musk-oxen on the island, and not far from here? I
must see them. I'll have the time because it won't
dry up for a day or two, and I don't have to sit
around and just wait for it to happen, I said to myself.

I drew the picture of a musk-ox and showed it to Andrew. He understood that I wanted to know the name for it in his tongue.

"Umingmak," he said, and I added another word to my picture dictionary.

"You ... and me ... go see?" I emphasized and pointed south.

He shook his head, and that was all. I assumed that he understood what I asked, but did not want to come along.

Chuck had been right. There were musk-oxen — nine adults and two calves. The many hours it took me to find them however, severely taxed my strength and determination. I sloshed through frigid slush and dragged myself over bare, soggy ground, the mud clinging to my mukluks. With pounding heart I crept up shaly slopes to lay prone on reaching their crests and to discover yet another slope, another crest.

The view was far. The haze, resembling an elevated, tranquil sea, lay below me and above it the snow-covered land dazzled. The sun was warm, invigorating.

The musk-oxen were on a bare patch of ground. Some grazed, others were lying down chewing their cud. I was sure that they had seen me a long way off, for there was nothing between them and me I could have used to conceal my approach. But they seemed to be curious rather than alarmed.

I got to within fifty feet or so before one of them
showed annoyance. It was a bull — their leader perhaps. He advanced a few steps, snorted and rubbed
his head against a foreleg. It was the same movement
one of the four I had met at Fielder Point had made.
As then, I took it as a warning not to come any
closer and backed up a few feet. Immediately, he
calmed down. He had the looks of an age-old, but im-
posing creature. Strands of his dark, shirt-like fur
almost reached the ground. Umingmak means: 'the long-
haired one', and it was to the point.

The bull was really magnificent and so were the
other bulls and cows. Meeting each separately, I
would have been hard pressed to distinguish between
them. The exception was the two calves. Though they
resembled their parents: a grayish muzzle, white
stockings, a pale-yellow saddle, their fur was curly,
lacking the long hairs, and they sported no horns.
Their faces wore an almost pouting expression that
reminded me of spoiled brats.

For a long time I viewed the herd from every side,
and would have gone on doing so had not the unexpected
happened. Suddenly, several of the musk-oxen snorted;
there was short milling and jostling, then all faced
away from me. At a distance a wolf loped across the
plateau. And as sudden as the musk-oxen had changed
from tranquillity to alertness, as suddenly the wolf

stopped, peered, then trotted at the herd. It had
come downwind, and there was no doubt in my mind that
the musk-oxen had smelled it long before it had
scented them. What incredible sense of smell these
wild creatures have, I thought and realized, once
again, what inferior senses nature has bestowed upon
man, for I had perceived no other scent than the
musk-oxen's.

Several times the wolf stopped and peered until it
was close to the herd where it halted, stood and
watched. There was a measure of arrogance, of threat
in its behavior. Nevertheless, its closeness gave me
the opportunity to have a good look at it. A male, I
was sure, standing at least three feet at the shoulder,
it had the appearance of a large German shepherd dog.
But its head was broad, blunt with a heavy muzzle and
short ears. The eyes were slanted and yellow. Its
coat was thick and of grayish white. It certainly
was a splendid specimen of canine, giving me the impression of a powerful, intelligent animal.

What evidently was a standoff between two natural
enemies lasted but short time. The wolf, as if test-
ing the musk-oxen's reaction, advanced a few steps.
Immediately, these massive, shaggy creatures became
uneasy, milled shortly and then, to my utter surprise,
wheeled and stampeded, the wolf after them. I watched
till they were out of sight. Then I turned back to
camp.

Our camp sat on slightly sloping ground that
drained well, and two days after my return from view-
ing the musk-oxen the ground was firm enough that an
aircraft with big tires could land and take off without getting bogged down in mud.

"Chuck will pick you up right away. We have been
waiting for your call, — over," the dispatcher said
when I reported my observation.

The sky was overcast and a brisk wind blew. As if
bewitched, a short time after I had contacted Isachsen,
the wind died down and thick fog moved in. We could
not see anything beyond fifty paces. Disappointed, I
reported the change in weather.

"Stand by. I'll call Chuck. He left just minutes
ago, — over," the dispatcher replied, and after a
while he informed me that Chuck had turned around and
was standing by till further notice.

"I'll give you a shout as soon as the fog lifts, —
over and standing by," I transmitted.

While Andrew and I waited for the fog to lift we
continued our language lesson. By now we both had
memorized many words in each other's tongue, and we
used them in our verbal exchanges. Neither he nor I
could form complete sentences — we just put together
words we knew would express certain things, desires
or remarks about observations. Our mutual jargon
might have sounded hilarious to listeners-in whose

tongue was either Eskimo or English and might have confused them, but we did not have that problem. And so, as Andrew got up and said: "Me go ... eat dog," I was not shocked or thought that he would attempt to eat a dog, but understood that he was going to feed the dogs. I chuckled because I fancied seeing surprised, possibly horrified expressions on the faces of white spectators.

But as many intentions are delayed or even completely altered by sudden circumstances, so was his intention to feed the dogs delayed.

The fog had lifted somewhat, making it possible to see as far as about half a mile.

"Taku! Nanuk!" he exclaimed and pointed.

On several occasions I had observed that when he was excited or taken by surprise by some action or observation, he expressed himself invariably in his native tongue. So did I, for I asked: "Where?" and not: "Nani?", as he had taught me.

Not more than a few hundred yards away ambled a big bear on the ice. Andrew ran to get his rifle, then ran onto the ice. I forgot the long hours of waiting for the weather to improve, and I did not bother to stand by the radio for messages — I watched the hunt.

I thought I had never seen a polar bear of such colossal size before, but then remembered the one I

had been confronted with when I had checked out the
recording spread, and wondered now if it was the
same.

At first, the bear did not see Andrew and continued his nonchalant amble. But all of a sudden he
reared up, peered in his direction, then dropped on
all four and galloped off. Andrew fell on one knee
and took aim with the rifle. Yet after a few tense
moments he lowered the weapon. The bear was already
out of range for a crippling or killing shot. A
short time after I lost sight of him — he had disappeared behind a ridge of ice. I was glad that this
short hunt ended with no bear dead. We needed no
meat for the dogs, and Andrew had several bear skins
to be proud of. Apparently, he felt the same.

"Me ... much nanurak," he said, what meant: "I
have many bear skins."

"Pitaliâluk ... plenty," I returned.

Whenever I used words in his tongue I also said
the corresponding English word. It helped him to
understand better because I often mispronounced the
particular word.

Back in camp, he fed the dogs with the rest of the
seal carcass. He divided it into equal portions of
about six pounds each. As I had observed many times
before, their feeding manners was a ferocious act of
snarling viciously at each other, then gulping down

in frantic haste the piece of meat thrown their way,
for each dog was afraid that another could snatch it
from him.

A short time after Andrew had fed the dogs wind
sprung up and dispersed the fog. I hastened to report it to Isachsen. And an hour later Chuck asked
over the VHF radio: "What's your barometer and wind?",
and after I had told him, said, curtly: "Coming in."
Minutes later he landed the aircraft near the camp
where the ground had firmed up.

We loaded the instruments, our personal gear and
the dogs. The remaining items: tents, sleds, the
snowmobile and many more things, we decided to fetch
later. Getting the dogs into the cabin was a chore I
would gladly have left to someone else. When grabbed
by their collars some groveled, whined and struggled;
others growled menacingly and showed their fangs.
But whip handle or boot and a firm grip turned even
the more recalcitrant submissive. The last to be
hoisted on board was the lead-dog, 'Scarface'. He
had sat apart from his mates. Did any of them stray
or misbehave, he snarled or got up taking on a
threatening stance that kept the offender in check.
He really was master of the pack.

I climbed into the co-pilot's seat. After the
takeoff I turned around, parted the curtain, separat-
ing cockpit and cabin, and peered into the latter.

A stench issued from it that almost made me puke. The
dogs had become airsick, had vomited and defecated.

"For heaven's sake ... open your window ... and
close that curtain ... I'm getting sick!" Chuck stammered.

He yanked a bag from his door-pouch and threw up
into it. A whiff of exhaust gas from the engine saved
me from doing the same. The stench did not affect
Andrew. He sat motionless in a corner of the cabin,
and I wondered whether he was asleep.

Chuck and I did not help to unload the aircraft at
Isachsen. Eskimos, smiling brightly, attended to it.
I saw only a few frown and take a step or two backward when Andrew opened the cargo door and called a
greeting in their tongue.

I went to report our arrival to the operations
manager. He was very kind and understanding, but
seemed to have a breathing problem, for he was catching his breath with obvious difficulty. He asked me
about the state of my health, jotted down my reply,
then commended me on my performance in the field.

"I s'pose you would like to take a shower and
change into your Sunday best," he said with a smile
on his clean-shaven, pale face.

Nothing else could have pleased me more. My enthusiastic response he accepted with: "That's all
right," and then told me that shower and meals were

available at the weather station.

He accompanied me to the door and showed me the way.

"He'll catch cold if he stays much longer in shirt-sleeves under that door," I muttered while I stepped through deep mud toward the entrance of the station. It did not enter my head that I had stunk up his office with the odor of seal and dog and bear and of myself, an unkempt human being.

I took a shower, hot and long-lasting and using much soap. Then I stood in front of the mirror and mused what name Nelly would call me this time. On other occasions, when I had returned after months of living and working in remote country, she had called me: "My wild man from the outdoors."

I donned freshly laundered clothes — washing and drying machines were there for personal use, and I had used them while I had taken the shower.

Then I headed for the dining room where I treated myself to fresh salads, a huge T-bone steak with fries and all the trimmings, and apple pie with ice cream on top. I drank coffee sweetened with sugar, and orange juice. It was a feast, indeed.

I saw new faces — guys from the weather station — was the target of furtive glances, and heard sly remarks about an aircraft whose cabin had to be scrupped and deodorized before the pilot and possible

225

passengers were safe from becoming nauseated.

After I had eaten I went in search of Andrew. I found him in company of Edgar, Ekaksak and the Eskimos who had helped unload the aircraft. He was showing them the bear skins.

"My friend ... tagvawutit," I said and proffered my right.

"Tâwâwutit ... friend," he returned while we shook hands.

(Tagvawutit means: good-bye to those who stay behind, whereas tâwâwutit means: good-bye to those who leave).

One of the Eskimo said something, and all smiled.

"Did you understand?" Edgar asked.

I shook my head.

"He said: you speak funny, but sounds similar to Eskimo."

"You think so, too?" I asked in return.

"Well," he drawled, then added: "But you try and that's good."

"Thanks, Edgar," I said and left, waving good-bye to all.

I picked up my gear and deposited it at the bunk assigned to me by the manager. And I ran into George. He was heading for the station.

"I haven't taken a shower yet," he said, and hurried on. I wondered where he had been all this time.

Then I met the gang. They kidded me about feeding dogs shortly before airlifting them, about stinking up someone's office, and having again the looks of a human, though a wild one. After more harmless banter they asked me to narrate my adventures on the ice.

I told about the near fatal encounters with bears, the dangerous ice I had traveled over, the hunting of seal and bear. The wolves, the caribou, the musk-oxen. The ice pack, leads, storms, I mentioned shortly because they themselves had encountered them, too.

I did not tell that I had experienced that heart-probing, fiery sense of loneliness when in danger, which sometimes had assailed my courage — a solitary man in unexplored and remote country — and that the sight of a human's face had been a profound relief.

Neither did I tell that regardless all the adventures I had experienced, the arctic land had cast its spell upon me, and though I was glad to go home, to civilization, I would return, thereby inflicting, not only to myself, but to Nelly, too, the sufferings of separation, the anxiety over the other's welfare and whereabout — that this was a curse.

"You sure had some rough times out there," Tony remarked after I stopped speaking. I had said all I wanted them to know.

Leon grinned. "You got that wrong. Just look at

him. Anybody must get scared seeing him ... even
bears," he said. He was referring to my mop of long
hair and frowsy beard and mustache, which I had not
trimmed.

"You look scary yourself," Bill teased. "But then,
we all could use some improvement in looks, couldn't
we?"

"Kidding apart, I think you were a lucky cuss,
after all," Norman said to me, and everyone present
agreed.

And that summed it up — at least for them.

Next day it snowed and fog shrouded the country.
It lasted till noon of the following day, and then
spring-like conditions returned.

Chuck and I flew to Thor Island and in two flights
recovered all the equipment we had left there.
Teddy's snowmobile, heavy and unwieldy, was the only
piece we disassembled before we could load it into
the aircraft.

Two more days I stayed in Isachsen. Then I bid
farewell to all who had been involved in the survey,
and flew in a DC-6 to Calgary's airport. There I
sent I telegram to Nelly — we had no telephone in our
cabin — bidding her to come to the Crossroad Hotel
where I would check in.

Then I hired a taxi. The cabby drove short distance and then stopped.

228

"You sonuvabitch! You stink! Get out!" he ordered,
startling me.

"I was ... that is ... I had ...." I stammered, and
then stopped speaking because he repeated: "Get out!"

I regained my wits. "Won't you listen for a moment?" I asked and since he did not repeat: "Get out!"
I told him where I had been, how I had lived, and for
how long.

He stared at me. "Is that true?" he demanded at
length, and as I replied: "I wouldn't lie", he said:
"I guess, that entitles you to a ride," and drove me
to the hotel, though with open windows.

The extra money I gave him to buy deodorant with,
pleased him, and he forgave me for: "Stinking up his
cab," as he put it.

Having experienced the cabby's reaction to the apparently offensive odor of my person, I halfway expected to be told to look for accommodations somewhere
else. But the clerk, handing me the registration
card to be filled in, was tactful, for he asked:
"Where d'you come from?" and then added: "Don't feel
offended, but you have a peculiar smell."

I told him where I had been.

"I should have known. We often have cowboys here."
I wondered if he knew where the Arctic was.

The room he assigned to me contained among all
other amenities a large bathroom with shower and bath-

tub, the latter being the thing I had wished for at
Isachsen, but for hygienics were not installed.

I took several baths now; each almost scalding and
soapy, to rid myself of the odor I could not detect,
but had insulted the cabby's nose and had induced the
clerk to classify me as cowboy.

About five hours later Nelly arrived by car. Upon
entering the room, she sniffed the air and then exclaimed: "How wonderful! You brought me seal skins!"

(She knew the smell because I had brought her seal
skin kamiks when I had returned from Baffin Island
the previous autumn).

I hesitated for a moment.

"No ... I didn't ... I couldn't," I then said, and
sniffed my arms. And there it was: the smell of seal
I had tried to get rid off. I realized now that eating seal blubber had saturated my body with what could
be called a fishy odor, and that neither scented soap
nor hot water would rid me of it. Time alone would
do it.

Her bluish eyes began to sparkle.

"Don't worry ... I don't mind the smell," she
humored and laughed, softly.

Later she trimmed my hair, beard and mustache.

"I won't cut off much because I like you to look a
bit wild," she kidded.

"Just wild?" I teased.

"You're the explorer. You can find out," she returned, a playful tone in her alto voice.

The change in climate — from arctic spring to prairie summer — was too abrupt for me to feel comfortable; I perspired profusely and felt like I was suffocating.

Therefore, after a few days of visiting friends in Calgary and neighboring area, we left the city for the Rocky Mountains where it was cool, and where I felt more at ease. We did some hiking and climbing, and within a week I felt well again. We returned to our home, the cabin in the woods nine miles east of Edmonton.

ISBN 1552124088-8